Decoding the
BIBLE
CODE

JOHN WELDON
with Clifford and Barbara Wilson

HARVEST HOUSE PUBLISHERS
Eugene, Oregon 97402

Unless otherwise indicated, verses are taken from the New American Standard Bible, © 1960, 1962, 1963, 1968, 1971, 1972, 1973, 1975, 1977 by the Lockman Foundation. Used by permission.

Verses marked KJV are taken from the King James Version of the Bible.

Cover by Terry Dugan Design, Minneapolis, Minnesota.

DECODING THE BIBLE CODE
Copyright © 1998 by Harvest House Publishers
Eugene, Oregon 97402

Library of Congress Cataloging-in-Publication Data
  Weldon, John.
      Decoding the Bible Code / John Weldon with Clifford & Barbara Wilson.
      p. cm.
      ISBN 1-56507-893-4
      1. Drosnin, Michael. Bible code. 2. Ciphers in the Bible—Controversial literature.
  3. Bible. O.T.—Prophecies—Data processing 4. Bible. O.T.—Data processing.
  I. Wilson, Clifford A. II. Wilson, Barbara, Dr. III. Title.
  BS647.2.D763W45 1998
  221.6'8—dc21   97-42829
                                                                        CIP

Printed in the United States of America.

98 99 00 01 02 /BP/ 10 9 8 7 6 5 4 3 2 1

*To Dr. John and Darlene Ankerberg
for their friendship, dedication to
the truth, and perseverance.*

Acknowledgments

John Weldon would especially like to thank Drs. Clifford and Barbara Wilson for their valuable input, role, and encouragement in the writing of this book. As they know, it would not have been done without them.

Also, thanks to Lulu Williams for her word processing skills, and to Steve Miller for his excellent editorial work at Harvest House Publishers.

Contents

If the codes are proved to be genuine—and as yet some of today's greatest scientific minds have been unable to disprove them—they would be tantamount to scientific proof of the existence of God.

—Dr. Jeffrey Satinover
Cracking the Bible Code (cover)

1

Introducing the Bible Code

I t's either the most incredible discovery in the history of the world or one of the most spurious. Allegedly, the Bible contains a secret code that details the entire life of every person in the past, present, and future, and gives a record of all world events, including natural disasters.

What is this marvelous code and how does it work? The hidden code involves a "skip sequence" of Hebrew letters that is said to spell out the details of human history. Supposedly, an omniscient intelligence somehow coded the Bible in such a manner that this skip code could be discovered only in our modern computer age.

The Search for a Code

Computers aside, the concept of a hidden Bible code is almost as old as the Bible itself. The possibility that such a code might exist has fascinated Jews, Christians, occultists, the plain curious, and even the famous. Sir Isaac Newton was reportedly among the latter:

> The first modern scientist, the man who figured out the mechanics of our solar system and discovered the force of gravity, Sir Isaac Newton, was certain there was a hidden code in the Bible that would reveal the

future. He learned Hebrew, and spent half his life trying to find it. In fact, it was for Newton, according to his biographer John Maynard Keynes, an obsession. When Keynes became provost at Cambridge University, he discovered there the papers that Newton had packed up in 1696 when he retired as provost. Keynes was shocked.

Most of the million words in Newton's own handwriting were not about mathematics or astronomy, but esoteric theology. They revealed that the great physicist believed there was hidden in the Bible a prophecy of human history. Newton, said Keynes, was certain that the Bible, indeed the whole universe, was a "cryptogram set by the Almighty," and wanted to "read the riddle of the Godhead, the riddle of past and future events divinely fore-ordained." Newton was still searching for the Bible code when he died. But his lifetime quest failed no matter what mathematical model he applied.

Newton never found a code because, proponents claim, the code could be discovered *only* by computer.[1] Code researcher Michael Drosnin explains:

The hidden text of the Bible was encoded with a kind of time-lock. It could not be opened till the computer had been invented. . . .

At its heart, it's a simple skip code in the existing text of the Old Testament. We find that if we [use a computer to] skip every five, or ten or hundred letters, hidden messages are revealed: the names of people who live today; the details of events that happened thousands of years after the Bible was written; dates, places, names, all in accurate detail.[2]

This concept of a code is influenced by and based in kabbalistic metaphysics and numerological theory. For example, Elijah ben Solomon (1720–97), also known as the Gaon (or

Genius) of Vilna, a leading Jewish mystic of the eighteenth century, is often cited as one who believed in the code. In part, he inspired three modern Jewish scholars, Eliyahu Rips, Doron Witztum, and Yoav Rosenberg, to spend years investigating the possibility of such a code. Finding initial compelling evidence of this code, they brought their discoveries to the attention of the academic community in 1988 and 1994. Then skeptical journalist Michael Drosnin expanded the code and popularized it for everyone else in mid-1997 in his smash bestseller *The Bible Code*, and several months later a more serious and technically oriented text was published by psychiatrist and code expert Dr. Jeffrey Satinover, entitled *Cracking the Bible Code*.

However, the principal code researchers claim that the popularization of the codes by Michael Drosnin and other popular treatments misrepresents and distorts the serious research and brings disrepute to the entire field. To date, the majority of people are familiar only with the popular treatments and have not been exposed to the scientific data that underlies the codes. For this reason we will address the popular treatments in some detail so that misconceptions may be cleared up. And, because the core evidence for the code is found in the work of Witztum, Rips, Rosenberg, and other principals, we will deal with that as well, for this, in a sense, is the material that will finally determine whether or not a code exists.

What we will discover in our analysis is that we are really dealing with two different approaches to a single phenomenon—assuming the code's legitimacy. If the code proves to be true, than we can find no immediate objection to the more conservative approach, which sees the code in evidential terms exclusively. In such a case, the only thing the code could tell us is that an omniscient power, presumably God, did author the Torah. The popular "divinatory" and message oriented approach (discussed later) would have to be considered an illegitimate application of the code from both the scientific and biblical perspectives.

The Astounding Claims

There is no doubt that the Bible code proponents are making astounding, even incredible claims. Taking only the initial "surface" level of the code that Rips, Witztum, and Drosnin are now dealing with, "apparently every major figure, every major event in world history, can be found with the level of encoding we already do know."[3]

What Rips and his colleagues did was to turn the entire Old Testament into one continuous strand of 304,805 computer-programmed letters. Once programmed, the computer searches in skip sequence for a key word or phrase—such as "Yitzhak Rabin" or "John Kennedy." When the computer finds the key word that it has been programmed to search for, it then looks for related words and information coded in close proximity to that word. "Time after time it has connected names, dates, and places encoded together. . . ."[4]

The Gulf War Predicted

In Drosnin's book, *The Bible Code*, the 1991 Gulf War is used as an example to illustrate how the code works: "We [Drosnin and Rips] asked the computer to search for Saddam Hussein. Then we looked for related words to see if they came together in a way that was mathematically significant. With the Gulf War, we found Scuds, Russian missiles, and the date the war would begin coded with the name Hussein."[5] Another way of using the code is to find key words or multiple uses of a word in the biblical text and then to search for a code related to these. For example:

> . . . Rips discovered an extremely large number, and proportion, of cases where, as he had surmised, *the topical theme for a given passage as represented by a single word in the surface text* (e.g., the word "Eden" in

> passages that discuss the Garden of Eden) *was echoed
> by an unusually large cluster of encoded appearances of
> that same word in that same passage*—more often than
> could reasonably be expected merely by chance. It
> was as though *this* paragraph had deliberately been
> written in such a way as to ensure that the "word
> cluster" could be extracted from it many times at
> many different equidistant letter skips.[6]

Considering what proponents claim the Bible code reveals, a phenomenon like this is either monumentally significant or monumentally flawed. We are dealing with either one of the greatest revelations in human history, or one of the greatest mistakes. Everyone who has heard the fascinating details of this code wants to know: Is the code real?

Rabin's Assassination and Other Startling Events

For example, what exactly does Drosnin claim the Bible code has predicted? It reads like a Who's Who of world personalities and events. Consider these examples. Allegedly the assassination of Yitzhak Rabin was revealed a year in advance, including the name of the assassin, and the place and year of the assassination. The code revealed the words "Yitzhak Rabin," "assassin who will assassinate," "Amir," "Tel Aviv," and "in 5756" (the Jewish calendar year for 1995–96). Clinton's election as president was revealed six months in advance by the words "Clinton" and "president." Watergate and Nixon's resignation were found in the words "Watergate," "who is he," and "president, but he was kicked out."

Here are some other examples of what apparently has been found coded in the Bible: the Great Depression of 1929; the moon landing, including the date Neil Armstrong stepped on the lunar surface, July 20, 1969; the collision of the Shoemaker-Levy comet with Jupiter, including the names of the astronomers who discovered the comet in 1993; the Jewish holocaust, including the terms "Hitler," "Nazi," "Berlin,"

"Eichmann," "ovens," and "extermination," as well as the gas used to kill the Jews ("Zyklon B"—encoded with the name Eichmann); "Roosevelt," "Churchill," and "Stalin"; the American Revolution in 1776; "Napoleon," "France," and "Waterloo"; the Ebola virus; the 1917 Communist Revolution in Russia; "Shakespeare" coded with "presented on stage," and his plays "Hamlet" and "Macbeth"; "Homer" is identified as "the Greek Poet"; "Beethoven" and "Johann Bach" are encoded as "German composers," along with "Mozart" who is encoded with "composer" and "music"; "Rembrandt" is encoded with "Dutch" and "painter"; "Picasso" is called "the artist"; the "Wright Brothers" are encoded with "airplane"; "Edison" is encoded with "electricity" and "light bulb"; "Marconi" is encoded with "radio"; "Newton" and "Einstein" are each encoded with their major discovery—"Newton" with "gravity" and "Einstein" with "he overturned present reality" and "theory of relativity"; the code also stated the month and year of the February 5, 1996 terrorist attack on Israel which killed 23 people, encoded with "autobus," "Jerusalem," "bombing," and "Jaffa Road."

The code is also said to have revealed the unexpected election of Prime Minister Netanyahu to the Israeli Government, along with "surely he will be killed." President Roosevelt's December 1941 Declaration of War is seen while "Pearl Harbor" is encoded with the words "destruction of the fortress," "the fleet," "World War," "December 7," and "Hiroshima." In addition, "atomic holocaust" is encoded with the year "1945."

The code spelled out the murders of Abraham Lincoln, Mahatma Ghandi, Anwar Sadat, and John Kennedy. With Kennedy, the words "President Kennedy to die" and "Dallas" were coded. It also revealed the name "Oswald" along with "marksman" and "sniper," and the fact that Kennedy would be killed in the head. In addition there was the name "Ruby" with "he will kill assassin." Even the assassination of Robert

F. Kennedy was found, along with the name "Sirhan" and "second ruler will be killed."

The code mentioned the February 1994 massacre of 30 Arabs praying at a famous Muslim mosque; including the name of the killer, "Goldstein," and "Hebron," where it occurred. For the Japanese Doomsday cult "Aum Shinrikyo" it included the words "subway," "plague," and "gas." The "Oklahoma bombing" had even more related information. It included the words "Oklahoma," "terrible, frightening death," and "there will be terror," along with "Murrah Building," and "killed," "torn to pieces." But there was also "his name is Timothy," "McVeigh," "day 19," "on the 9th hour," "in the morning" and "he ambushed," "he pounced," and "terror." The San Francisco earthquake and fire of 1906 are encoded with "S.F. Calif" and "1906" along with "fire," "earthquake," and "city consumed, destroyed."

Drosnin's *The Bible Code* also predicts major future events such as World War III and Armageddon.

Dr. Jeffery Satinover is an M.D. who has had "unprecedented access to the scholars and scientists most closely involved with the codes—both proponents and critics."[7] In addition to his expertise in mathematics, physics, laboratory science, and clinical psychiatry, he is a former Williams James lecturer in Psychology and Religion at Harvard and holds degrees from MIT, the Harvard Graduate School of Education, and the University of Texas. He is currently studying physics at Yale University. He believes the code research may involve "the most important scientific research ever undertaken" because "if the codes [are] genuine then this research [is] without exaggeration the most astounding scientific discovery—it sounds ridiculous to put it so bluntly, but there's no way around it—*ever.*"[8] He even hints that startling revelations are in the works: "Certain details are likely never to fully see the light of day, given the players involved. But others will in fact be presented when the time is right. Much of what I cannot say now, and have left out of this book, is very likely to see print soon. What I can discuss now is astonishing enough."[9]

In his more credible study, Dr. Satinover also provides examples of the kinds of things found in the Bible code. Although not as sensational as those of Michael Drosnin, they are striking nonetheless. For example, in the Genesis account of the Garden of Eden we find two sections of Scripture: one describing "seed-bearing plants" (Genesis 1:20–2:16) and the other trees having "seed-bearing fruit," which were given to mankind for food in the Garden (Genesis 2:7–3:3). According to Satinover, "all seven edible species of seed-bearing fruit in the land of Israel were found encoded in just that passage of text that alludes to them."[10]

Dr. Rips came to a more striking conclusion about the passage that mentioned the trees that bore edible fruit. He felt that within the passage he should be able to find the names of *every* tree in the Garden mentioned by Jewish tradition—25 in all. According to code researcher and mathematics professor Daniel Michelson:

> He took all 25 trees . . . and found them in the above chapter! Before the reader jumps out of his seat, let us explain that three- or four-letter words would normally appear at some intervals in a long segment as long as ours (about 1000 letters). What is so exceptional here is that most of the intervals [apart from chestnut and poplar] are very short. There is no other segment of Genesis of such length that contains so many trees at intervals less than 20.[11]

Related to the word "Hanukkah" (found embedded at a 261-letter interval), we have the terms "oil," "flask of oil," "menorah," "eight days," "twenty-fifth of Kislev," and so on— all terms directly related to the Jewish holiday that commemorates the uprising of the Jewish community during the Maccabean revolt.[12] In addition, another set of terms were arrayed around another Jewish holiday, that of Purim, including the name "Purim," its date, the "13th of Adar," the name "Mordecai," and the name and title "Queen Esther."[13] Witztum and his colleagues claim to have found *hundreds* of such arrays.

Satinover points out that the code even mentions common modern diseases such as diabetes—including the terms "diabetes," "ketones," "insulin," and "pancreas."[14] In addition, arrays related to AIDS involve such terms as "AIDS," "death," "in the blood," "annihilation," "in the form of a virus," "the HIV," "the immunity," "destroyed," "from Apes," plus many more.[15]

Among the correct terms found relating to the assassination of Egyptian president Anwar Sadat we find the following: "the conspiracy," "assassinate," "Sadat," "parade," "on the 8th of Tishri," "by the hand of a murderer," "1981," and also the assassin's first and last names, "Chaled" and "Islambooli."[16]

Concerning the Gulf War, we find the following terms: "SCUDS," "Russian," "missile," "Hussein," "Iraq," "Saddam," "3rd of Shevat," [First SCUD launched], "2nd of Shevat," [war began], "Schwartzkopf," "America," "in Saudi Arabia," "in Tel Aviv," "SCUD B," and so on.[17]

In relation to World War II and Hitler's attempt to destroy the Jewish people we find terms like "Eichmann," "in Auschwitz," "by the hand of the SS," "consumes," "gas," "Zyklon B," "one third of my people," "massacre," "Hitler," "nazi," "Berlin," and "in Germany."[18]

A Worldwide Fascination

Few things have captured the public's attention like the assertation that there are genuine codes hidden in the Bible. Oprah Winfrey devoted a large segment of one of her shows to the subject. Whenever the camera panned the audience, the viewer could see the people's intense interest in the subject—coupled with the fear that Drosnin's "Bible-based" predictions of approaching apocalyptic disasters just might be true. Warner Brothers quickly snapped up the film rights.

Drosnin himself is said to be working on a sequel. Other books are now in the works by other authors, including Doron Witztum, a co-author of the original article that stated the phenomenon had statistical credibility. By August 27, 1997, several months after *The Bible Code* was released, the Simon and Schuster web page had no less than 231 book reviews of Drosnin's book.

Why are millions of people fascinated with alleged Bible codes? Consider what the Bible codes phenomenon involves: a trinity of, respectively, the most respected, enticing, and frightening factors possible—the Bible, computer prediction of the future, and Armageddon. This certainly underscores the phenomenal success of Drosnin's text. *Time* magazine humorously noted, "The mix of Christian Scripture, Jewish mysticism, Cyberwizardry and existential dread is year 2000 catnip."[19]

There is enormous interest today in the Bible, with hundreds of millions of people worldwide viewing it as the Word of God. There is increasing interest and awe with the stunning capabilities of computers. Drosnin and Satinover both refer to the possible emergence of "quantum computers" that can perform in *minutes* calculations that would take our best supercomputers hundreds of *trillions* of years to perform. (In fact, to accomplish what a quantum computer could do in one *second* would require 10^{22} years [much more than trillions of years] on a standard computer!)

Finally, we have the ever-present, undying interest of people in the future—not only their own, but that of a world that seems to be inching closer to the brink than ever before.

The Bible code phenomenon wraps all of this into one intriguing and fascinating package. So it is hardly surprising to find Drosnin's *The Bible Code* on all the bestseller lists. One commentator noted there is a perennial urge to find order in the creation and divinity in order. This desire is as old as humanity and, in the words of British scholar John Bowker, editor of *The Oxford Dictionary of World Religions,* "profound in all religions."[20]

2

The Research
Behind the Code

> We conclude that the proximity of ELSs (Equidistant
> Letter Sequences) with related meanings in the Book
> of Genesis is not due to chance.

These words concluded an article in the prominent
review journal *Statistical Science* (August 1994) and
set the stage for a phenomenon that would influence
many millions of people worldwide.

The article, describing a startling, hidden code in the book
of Genesis, had undergone an extensive six-year review
process and it had passed with flying colors.

The three authors of the article were Israeli scientists—
Doron Witztum, Eliyahu Rips, and Yoav Rosenberg. Eliyahu
Rips is an associate professor of mathematics at the Hebrew
University of Jerusalem, a leading authority on the mathematics of quantum physics. Doron Witztum is a physicist and
computer specialist, and is said to be the preeminent codes
researcher in the world. Both men are recognized interna-
tionally for their achievements. In fact, Rips is considered a
near genius in the field of mathematics. Yoav Rosenberg is
associated with the Jerusalem College of Technology.

Setting Up the Experiment

Witztum explains the development of their research:

> According to mystical [Kabbalistic] sources in Jewish
> tradition, the Torah can be read and understood on
> many levels, including the level of a "hidden text."
> Twelve years ago, I developed a method to see if this
> hidden text could be scientifically and objectively val-
> idated. Professor Eliyahu Rips developed the mathe-
> matical system for measuring the statistical
> significance of the results. Yoav Rosenberg took
> Eliyahu's ideas and developed an appropriate com-
> puter program to carry out these experiments.[1]

What did these men find, and how did they find it? Keep
in mind that their curiosity was piqued by the eighteenth-
century Jewish mystic the Gaon of Vilna, who believed that all
the information that ever was or will be is encoded in the
Torah, the first five Books of the Bible. As a test, using the
Encyclopedia of Great Men in Israel (a standard Hebrew reference
text) they took the names of 34 of the most prominent Jewish
men who lived and died between the ninth and eighteenth
centuries. Using the normal Jewish way of abbreviating names,
they programmed the computer to search for these names.
They found encoded both the name and the date of each
prominent person's birth or death, with the numbers being
represented by letter equivalents in Hebrew because Old Testament Hebrew has no number symbols.[2] Using a method
known as Equidistant Letter Sequencing (ELS), they claim to
have demonstrated that the famous individuals' names and the
dates of their births or deaths were hidden in code in Genesis.

Doron Witztum explained the process with a word from
the twentieth century:

> The process is to take one central word, find its min-
> imal occurrence in the text, and then construct a
> tableau based on it. In this case, our topic is the death

camp Auschwitz. We take an objectively chosen list of related words. In this case, we are looking for the names of the sub-camps that comprised the Auschwitz complex. We make a tableau based on the words "of Auschwitz." With our tableau set, the computer will systematically look throughout the text for a minimal occurrence of each of the sub-camps. Any one of these words can appear anywhere in the text of Genesis. We find something very unexpected—that they consistently appear in the area of the words "of Auschwitz."[3]

Again, the research was apparently based on the theory of a highly influential eighteenth century Jewish sage and Kabbalist, Eliyyahu ben Shelomoh Zalman (Elijah ben Solomon), although the idea of a code goes back much further—at least to the twelfth century, and probably earlier. He believed that the Torah contained the history and future of the world in code form. In the early twentieth century a Jewish rabbi, H.M.D. Weissmandel, discovered that if he skipped 50 letters, another 50, then another 50, and so on, the word "Torah" was spelled out at the beginning of the book of Genesis, as well as Exodus, Numbers, and Deuteronomy.[4]

The Israeli scientists next used computers in their endeavor to see if a code actually existed.

How Equidistant Letter Sequences Work

How does ELS work? The text of Genesis was input into a computer and strung out as one lengthy letter sequence. Starting from the very first letter, the computer was programmed to find a specific word or phrase hidden in the text. In other words, it was programmed to find sequences of equally spaced letters—that is, to make skips of two letters, five letters, one hundred letters, and so on—until it finds the requested key word. Then it looks for associated words in close proximity to the key word. If significant word associations are found close enough together, the letters are compacted and the graph is drawn horizontally, diagonally, vertically, from right to left, or left to right. This provides the overall tableau format showing the coded information.

The Statistical Odds

What the authors of the article claim to have found is coded information that defies chance occurrence.

Understandably, the editors of *Statistical Science* were skeptical and requested that the experiment be repeated, using the names of another set of prominent men. The results were the same: the names and birth or death dates were found in close proximity in every case.

The statistical odds that their Bible code phenomena were genuine were placed at 99.998% for the first set. The odds that they were due to chance were less than .00002, or less than one chance in 50,000 (technically <1/62,500).[5] On both sets, the odds that they were due to chance were given as less than one in 2.5 billion.[6] (The results were reported officially only on the second set of names at the insistence of *Statistical Science* editors and referees as a buffer against possible inadvertent manipulation of data in the first set.) Regardless, Dr. Satinover tells us:

> The vast majority of scientific journals accept for publication papers whose hypotheses are validated at a significance level of 0.05 (1 chance in 20 that the results happened just by chance). Life-and-death medical decisions may require odds of 1 in 50. Because the ELS phenomenon was so strange—and its implications so vast, were it accurate—the editor and referees at *Statistical Science* raised the bar to publication to 1 in 1000 (in line with the suggestions of Professors Kazhdan, Piateski-Shapiro, Bernstein and Furstenberg, quoted earlier). The results bettered even that by more than sixty times.[7]

In fact, the authors had done similar research that was documented in an earlier paper published in the premier *Journal of the Royal Statistical Society* (1988). The authors found startling word-pair associations, some 300 in all, the chance configuration of which Satinover placed at less than one in 50 quadrillion.[8]

Michael Drosnin, a highly skeptical bestselling author and former reporter for the *Washington Post* and *Wall Street Journal*, learned of the phenomenon. Intrigued, but retaining his skepticism, he set out to investigate the research and eventually became convinced that it was for real. He then devised his own extended code, and published his discoveries in *The Bible Code*.

Evaluating the Results

Consider what we have here: a startling phenomenon with monumental implications first published in the eminent *Journal of the Royal Statistical Society* (1988). The odds are one in 50 quadrillion that the phenomenon occurs solely by chance. A related phenomenon is subsequently published with new data in *Statistical Science: A Review Journal of the Institute of Mathematical Statistics* (1994), another eminent journal. The experiment is run twice and stands. For this set of data, the odds are one in 2.5 billion the phenomenon could have occurred by chance. Keep in mind that the review process took six years. Witztum says,

> [In this] rigorous six-year process of review and analysis . . . several referees checked the work and asked for further testing. One of these involved rerunning the experiment with a completely fresh set of data, and also checking other control texts. This was done and the research passed all tests with very highly significant results.[9]

The editor of *Statistical Science,* Robert E. Kass of Carnegie-Mellon University, said the following in a prefatory note:

> Our referees were baffled: their prior beliefs made them think the Book of Genesis could not possibly contain meaningful references to modern-day individuals, yet when the authors carried out additional analyses and checks the effect persisted.[10]

The phenomenon, which, if true, would seem to be proof of the divine inspiration of the Torah, is then *positively* reviewed in a *liberal* theological journal.[11] Then, in 1996–1997 the original authors repeat the experiment, using a critic's new improved set of data—and there are even more startling results.[12]

Words from the Convinced

So far, the results have been critiqued and supported by leading mathematical scholars from Harvard and Yale universities, as well as the Hebrew University of Jerusalem. Initially all the scholars were skeptics, and understandably, they concluded conservatively:

> The present work represents serious research carried out by serious investigators. Since the interpretation of the phenomenon in question is enigmatic and controversial, one may want to demand a level of statistical significance beyond what would be demanded for more routine conclusions. The results obtained are sufficiently striking to deserve a wider audience and to encourage further study.[13]

The research was also critiqued and endorsed by Dr. Andrew Goldfinger, a senior research physicist at Johns Hopkins University in Baltimore, and by former skeptic Harold Gans, a retired highly placed expert code analyst who formerly worked as a senior cryptologic mathematician at the National Security Agency in the U.S. Department of Defense. According to Drosnin,

> Harold Gans had spent his life making and breaking
> codes for American Intelligence. He was trained as a
> statistician. He spoke Hebrew. And he was sure that
> the Bible Code was "off-the-wall, ridiculous." Gans
> was certain he could prove the Code did not exist. He
> wrote his own computer program, and he looked for
> the same information the Israelis had found. He was
> surprised. It was there. The dates that the sages were
> born and died were encoded with their names.[14]

In fact, Gans was so skeptical that, after confirming the
results of the initial study (finding the Jewish sages' names
and dates of birth and/or death in the Hebrew text of Genesis), he tried to disprove everything through a second test:

> Gans could not believe it. He decided to look for
> entirely new information in the Bible Code, and
> thereby expose the flaw in Rips' experiment, possibly
> even reveal a hoax. "If this was real," said Gans, "then
> I figured the cities where these men were born and
> died ought to be encoded as well.[15]

In the end, he actually found that Genesis had also
encoded the respective *cities* of birth or death! In a public
statement Gans wrote, "The statistical results obtained were
even stronger than that obtained for the first experiment."
And "after exhaustive analysis, I have reached the conclusion
that the codes discovered in Genesis . . . exist, and the probability that they are mere coincidence is vanishingly small."
(See note 16, pp. 168-69).

While people are free to disagree with the conclusions of
the scholars who have rigorously tested the Bible code, they
cannot dispute their credentials. Gans, for example, is a bril-
liant mathematician who has published over 190 technical
papers, most of them classified. "He had won the coveted
Meritorious Civilian Service Award for heading up a team of
mathematicians, cryptanalysts, programmers, and engineers
in solving a high-priority problem considered virtually

uncrackable."[17] In addition, at first he was a skeptic who thought the claims were absurd. For almost three weeks, day and night (for a total of 440 hours), Gans had his computer examine all possible variations of combinations of the 78,000 Hebrew letters in the book of Genesis. His computer program checked hundreds of thousands of possible letter combinations at many different intervals.[18]

The results made a convert out of Gans, who now teaches classes in synagogues worldwide, alleging that the codes prove the divine Authorship of the Torah. The Aish HaTorah Discovery Seminar (Aish HaTorah is a rabbinical college in the Old City of Jerusalem) sponsors an international educational program designed to reinterest secular Jews in traditional Judaism and the Torah, and includes information about the Bible code in the seminars.

Many former critics now agree with the response that Dr. Jeffrey Satinover gave to those who were skeptical of his initial positive codes article in *Bible Review*:

> The robustness of the Torah Codes findings derives from the rigor of the research. To be published in a journal such as *Statistical Science*, it had to run, without stumbling, an unusually long gauntlet manned by some of the world's most eminent statisticians. The results were thus triply unusual: in the extraordinariness of what was found, in the strict scrutiny the findings had to hold up under; and in the unusually small odds (less than one in 62,500) that they were due to chance. Other amazing claims about the Bible, Shakespeare, etc., have never even remotely approached this kind of rigor, and have therefore never come at all close to publication in a peer-reviewed hard-science venue. The editor of *Statistical Science*, himself a skeptic, has challenged readers to find a flaw: though many have tried, none have succeeded. All the "First Crack" questions asked by *Bible Review* readers—and many more sophisticated ones—

have therefore already been asked by professional critics and exhaustively answered by the research. Complete and convincing responses to even these initial criticisms can get very technical.[19]

Even the most respected mathematician in Israel, a former skeptic, became convinced. On March 19, 1996, Robert J. Aumann told the Israeli Academy of Science, "The Bible code is an established fact."[20]

Aumann, one of the world's experts in game theory, a member of both the Israeli and U.S. Academy of Science, said, "It's very important to treat this like any other scientific experiment—very cold, very methodological, you test it, and you look at the results—as far as I can see the Bible Code is simply a fact."[21] "I am talking as an accountant, I have checked the books and it is Kosher. It's not just Kosher, it's Glatt Kosher."[22] Aumann added, "It's so different from anything known to science, there has been nothing like it in all the hundreds of years of modern science."[23]

Later, an Israeli mathematician, skeptical of the results, challenged the original Witztum/Rips experiment, claiming that there were certain inexactitudes that nullified the results. As noted, Rips and Witztum accepted this challenge and did the entire experiment all over again in December 1996, and January 1997, using the new data supplied by the skeptical mathematician. The results were "twenty times better than in the original experiment."[24]

In fact, in their original article, they claim anyone can personally verify their results: "In the Appendix, sufficient details are provided to enable the reader to repeat the computations precisely, and so to verify their correctness. The authors will provide, upon request, at cost, diskettes containing the program used in the texts G, I, R, T, U, V, W. . . ."[25]

Apparently, some former skeptics have done just that.

Words from the Critics

On the other hand, critics—especially rationalists and materialists—claim the results are "absurd," "nonsense," and "numerological rubbish." One critic reflects the dismay of many when he writes,

> It is disturbing that a number of eminent mathematicians have put their reputations on the line in support of the ELS nonsense. Among them are two members of the Israel Academy of Arts and Sciences, both winners of the Israel Prize and members of the U.S. National Academy of Sciences. Another is a member of the U.S. National Academy of Sciences and a winner of the MacArthur Award. Several other equally distinguished mathematicians, including a member of the Knesset, the Israeli parliament, round out the list.[26]

Another critic wrote, "It's going to take a bit more than a handful of buzzwords, some probabilistic calculations of an extremely narrowly defined experiment, and a lay author's glib statements that the computer science and the mathematics are flawless to convince me."[27]

According to Dr. Jeffrey Satinover, the response to the codes is rarely in the middle:

> The authors note with disappointment, but not surprise, that responses so far have mostly fallen into two categories: a prior acceptance or a prior rejection. The former, by believers and enthusiasts (especially those without mathematical training), is indeed not surprising. But the latter is—or should be. Since to date no one has discovered a flaw in the authors' work, it is reasonable to ask of scientifically trained, prior skeptics (who are certain these results must be a fluke), "What standard of proof would you accept as an indication that the phenomenon might be

genuine?" The most frequent answer by far is, *"There is no standard. I will not believe it regardless."*[28]

One academic critique of the codes was published by Dror Bar-Natan (a renowned quantum field theorist at Hebrew University), Alec Gindis, Arieh Levitan, and Brendan McKay (a world-class probabalist and computer specialist at the Australian National University). According to Eliyahu Rips, in his technical critique of their work, "The results and conclusions given in this report are invalid. . . . The experiments were performed with flawed data, which renders the reported results and conclusions invalid."[29]

In apparently another study, posted on the internet, Brendan McKay and Dror Bar-Natan attempted to replicate the initial work and, claiming highly technical problems in the experiment, failed to find any trace of the claimed phenomena: "No indication of any extraordinary phenomenon was found."[30] Rips has responded to the criticisms of McKay, saying, "I think he is not right." But even if McKay were correct (according to expert Robert J. Aumann), for particular reasons, the experiment would still be valid.[31] Further, when the errors in both the critics' and principals' data are corrected, the results are said to turn out more strongly in favor of the Bible code.[32]

Critics claim they can disprove the *Statistical Science* article, although in almost three years no one has done so. Doron Witztum's new book will detail the results of many new experiments, which he says are even more striking. In his June 4, 1997 public statement, Witztum declared: "We have conducted seven other experiments that are available as pre-prints. At present, I am completing a book that gives a true view of this fantastic phenomenon, and that will describe not only the ten experiments I mentioned, but also many other successful experiments which reveal a vast spectrum of subjects, ancient and modern."

Regardless, "Statisticians continue to hope for a crack in the experiment. Kass, executive editor of *Statistical Science*, suggests the authors may have subconsciously biased their results by selectively reporting their findings. 'Every statistician I know has reacted that the most likely explanation is that some kind of selection or "tuning" of the method did take place, though the authors may not be conscious of it,' he says."[33]

The Need for Closer Scrutiny

It is generally agreed that outstanding claims require outstanding proofs. The serious Bible codes research of Rips and others will be proved genuine if it can withstand final technical scrutiny. Certainly for the research to have survived for this long would seem to limit our conclusions. Either the code phenomenon is invalid, and, for reasons unknown, very competent reviewers and critics never saw the flaws. Or it is valid, at least for the version of the Torah that was used in the experiments.

In the remaining chapters we will continue to examine the codes phenomenon. Again, to date, the work of Rips and other scholars remains unrefuted, suggesting at least the possibility of a genuine code. Drosnin's work, however, is in a different category. As a popular text that did not employ scientific controls, it is much more vulnerable to criticism. Regardless, we will see that, for the Bible code research as a whole, we seem to remain on the horns of a dilemma. On the one hand for textual and other reasons, the phenomenon "cannot" exist. On the other hand, the phenomenon seems to have been demonstrated to the satisfaction of many leading statisticians and former skeptics.

What makes the research seemingly so significant is that the code examples cited earlier are only a few of literally hundreds of examples that are now said to be awaiting publication. According to Satinover, Witztum's new book will be the "definitive book on the subject" and will not only detail his methods in depth but provide "many hundreds of examples of great beauty."[34] Further, referring to Doron Witztum and his colleagues, Dr. Satinover asserts, "In the little over two-and-a-half years since their original publication [in *Statistical Science*] they have put together *seven new controlled experiments*, with highly significant results, all with very different data sets, all in light of the various criticisms and challenges that have been raised."[35]

Once this research is published and critics have had a chance to examine it in depth, publish their findings, and get a response from the principals—and this happens several times—then we will certainly know a great deal more about whether the Bible code is legitimate or not. But again, this will take a minimum of several years. In the meantime, the best approach we can advise is a wait-and-see perspective that recognizes both the incredible nature of the claims and the complex realities of the research.

3

Bible Numerology and the Bible Code

t best, Bible numerology has a checkered history, as indicated by the critical reviews and analyses of books that have been published in the last 200 years. Books promoting this subject have been less than rigorous from a critical standpoint, and characteristically have ended up allowing their numerologies to distort what the surface text actually teaches.[1] As the *Evangelical Dictionary of Theology* concludes, "Many elaborate efforts have been made to attach special meanings to numbers. But none are satisfactory."[2] The authoritative *Zondervan Pictorial Encyclopedia of the Bible* refers to "exegetical" biblical numerology as "magical nonsense," noting that its "gnostic exegesis contradicts the clear biblical principle in 2 Peter 1:20, which says 'that no prophecy of scripture is a matter of one's own interpretation.'"[3]

Before we proceed, let's take a brief but critical look at biblical numerology. Although the Bible code, with its skip sequences, is a unique form of biblical numerology to which standard criticisms do not necessarily apply, a general understanding of the subject and its problems will help us in our overall evaluation.

Understanding Biblical Numerology

The word *numerology* comes from the Latin *numerus* or "number" and *logy*, or "study," meaning "the study of numbers." A related term that has come into somewhat popular use is *numerics*, which can refer either to a general study of numbers or a specific evaluation of the alleged mysteries of numbers. The Bible clearly uses numbers in a conventional and rhetorical sense, and as far as these are concerned, the study of biblical numerology is legitimate.[4] We also occasionally find numbers used symbolically—such as the number 7 in Revelation 3:18[5]—but we never find numbers used mystically—that is, with hidden meanings that can illuminate the text or reveal the future.

Its Beginnings

The concept of symbolic and mystical numerology appears to have begun with the Greek philosopher Pythagoras (sixth century B.C.); however, some argue that Pythagoras himself derived it from the Jews. While he was an adept philosopher and mathematician, Pythagoras is equally well known for his speculations on reincarnation and cosmology, and he held to certain occult beliefs.

Its Influence

Symbolic and mystical numerology has long been the mainstay of the world of the occult (*see* Ankerberg, Weldon, *Encyclopedia of New Age Beliefs*, pages 145-51). Somewhat surprisingly, numerology in its symbolic and mystical forms, has also found a limited reception within the church since the earlier centuries of its existence. "With the rise of the Gnostic heresies came the concomitant growth of the pseudo-science of [numerological] Gematria. While biblical writers do not employ the system, Church Fathers were profoundly influenced by it, so much so, that they made it part of their apologetic."[6]

Of course not all the Fathers accepted it; some, such as Irenaeus, argued strongly against it, pointing out that it had no place in biblical hermeneutics:

> Irenaeus is an outstanding example of one who made valiant attempts to stop the tide of theological mysticism and allegorical interpretation which was popular in the early church. He recognized the dangers of such a system both as to method and result. He saw clearly that the method employed in this system was subjective, and therefore, of no value. . . . Irenaeus points out that in the study of numerics long hours were spent analyzing and praising the work of the artist (the Lord) and this was done to the neglect of the Artist Himself.[7]

As with the Bible code, the "biblical" numerology of the Gnostics seemed impressive, and even suggestive of divine origin. Yet it was ultimately unreliable:

> The Gnostics relied rather heavily on mystical numerology in support of their views. The numerological data presented by the Gnostics were indeed impressive and seemed to indicate that divine truth could be expressed and explained with such phenomena. In the light of this vast corpus of numerological data, Irenaeus raised the following question:
>
> > Is it a meaningless and accidental thing, that the positions of names, and the election of the apostles, and the working of the Lord, and the arrangement of created things, are what they are?
>
> Iranaeus answered his question in the negative, but quickly pointed out that no one should
>
> > . . . seek to prosecute inquiries respecting God by means of numbers, syllables, and letters. For this is an uncertain mode of proceeding, on account of their varied and diverse systems, and because every sort of hypothesis may at the present day be, in

like manner, devised by any one; so that they can derive arguments against the truth from these very theories, insomuch as they may be turned in many different directions. . . .

In *Against Heresies,* he takes the Gnostics to task for their perverse use of the number 5 to establish certain doctrines. His polemic is as follows:

Anyone, in fact, might collect many thousand other things of the same kind, both with respect to this number and any other he chose to fix upon, either from the Scriptures, or from the works of nature lying under his observation. But although such is the case, we do not therefore affirm that there are five Aeons above the Demiurge; nor do we consecrate the Pentad, as if it were some divine thing; nor do we strive to establish things untenable, nor ravings such as they indulge in by means of that vain kind of labor; nor do we perversely force a creation well adapted by God for the ends intended to be served, to change itself into types of things which have no real existence; nor do we seek to bring forward impious and abominable doctrines, the detection and overthrow of which are easy to all possessed of intelligence.[8]

Clearly, the Gnostics employed numerology in the same or a similar fashion as numerologists historically, and when it comes to the biblical text, they achieved the same result— that is, its distortion. As we will soon see, this is also what we find happening in many cases with the Bible code.

The Problems with Biblical Numerology

Perhaps the most influential biblical numerologists of relatively recent times have been Ivan Panin and E.W. Bullinger, whose materials remain in print today. Panin, a Roman Catholic, was the author of several texts: *Biblical*

Numerics (1911–12); *Scientific Demonstrations of the Inspiration of Scripture* (1924); *Biblical Chronology* (1934); and *The New Testament from the Greek as Established by Bible Numerics* (1935). Bullinger wrote *Numbers in Scripture* (1895). In his *Biblical Numerology: A Basic Study of the Use of Numbers in the Bible*, theologian John J. Davis provides a critique of the biblical numerology of Bullinger and Panin, showing that they are, in essence, useless as to apologetic value or as a means of more accurately interpreting the text. In terms of apologetic value, biblical numerology does not in any manner prove or even supply legitimate evidence of the divine inspiration of the Bible, nor can it be used, as proponents allege, to determine the autographs. More recent biblical numerologists include Jerry Lucas and Del Washburn in their *Theomatics: God's Best-Kept Secrets Revealed* (1977), and they run into the same problems as well.[9]

In essence, biblical numerology to date has not proven its worth. It is far too subjective, speculative, and even contradicts itself in many places. In addition, when serious or fatal problems develop for a system of biblical numerology, ad hoc explanations are created in an effort to save the system when, instead, the proponents ought to recognize the futility of creating such systems.[10] Panin actually attempted to correct the Greek text to conform to his numerology!

Dr. Davis points out that the modern proponents of biblical numerology rarely, if ever, acknowledge the gnostic or mystical sources of their beliefs. "No credit is ever given to Pythagoras, the Talmudic or Cabalastic [sic] literature from which their methodology is derived. In fact, as one reads their works, he is constantly reminded of the fact that what they are proposing is new and unique."[11] But, in fact, "The mathematical procedures are precisely those of the Pythagoreans and the Gnostics. The only difference is that the conclusions are changed in order to conform to Christian theology."[12]

According to Dr. Davis, the proponents of biblical numerology give certain impressions: first, that the numerical values have always been associated with Greek and Hebrew letters; second, that they have made a startling new discovery; and third, that numbers have always had either symbolic or theological values. None of this is true:

> This whole system of exegesis operates upon the assumption that the Greek and Hebrew alphabets always had numeric values attached to them. It is at this point that the whole system breaks down. . . . the earliest traces of associating numerical values with the letters of the alphabet belonged to the Greeks of the sixth century B.C.[13]

Another problem is that large parts of important Bible passages are bereft of any observable numerical phenomena. In other words, if, as the argument goes, the proof of inspiration of the Bible depends on its mathematical structure, then we would have to conclude that most of the Bible is not inspired.

Ultimately, the biblical numerologist can find almost endless meanings in Scripture and pretty much anything he wants to find. And often, the very same methodology that numerologists use to reach positive conclusions can also be used to *disprove* those same conclusions!

Thus there is no doubt that Dr. Davis is correct when he writes that biblical numerologists "have blurred the very image they intended to clarify" and that "superficial exegesis is characteristic of those who indulge in mystical numerology."[14] For example, consider the 153 fishes mentioned by the apostle John in John 21:11. Why this specific number is given is unknown, but there is no biblically based reason for assuming some kind of special hidden meaning or significance. In fact, almost two dozen *different* interpretations have been offered by biblical numerologists for this single verse![15] (Davis cites 18 examples as given in J.A. Emerton, "The One

Hundred and Fifty Three Fishes in John 21:11," *The Journal of Theological Studies,* April 1958). Harold Camping, in his embarrassing book *1994,* actually concluded that Christ would return in 1994 based, in part, on this number of fishes![16]

Davis points out that numerology "is based on a false premise" because there is no evidence that Hebrews of the Old Testament attached numerical values to their alphabet. Thus, "the whole system must be rejected as a valid means of exegesis." He states,

> This system of interpretation contributes nothing to a better understanding of the text. If anything, it complicates the simplicity of the Word of God. Any method of interpretation that operates on a subjective notion is a scheme, not a system, and has no real place in the methods of hermeneutics.[17]

The Bible's Silence Over Numerology

If biblical numerology were as important as its proponents claim, one would have expected, as for the Bible code, that the Bible would have told us so. But nowhere in Scripture do we find even the slightest hint that symbolic or mystical biblical numerology is acceptable. Not a single New Testament writer ever pointed back to the significance of a symbolic or mystical number that occurred in the Old Testament—not one. This is a strange omission indeed if biblical numerology is as important as its proponents allege.[18] Davis concludes:

> The Bible does not use numbers in a mystical sense. There is no evidence that the letters of the alphabet were used to convey numerical values along with theological concepts. . . . When numbers and/or letters of the alphabet are given mystical or theological values there is no end to speculations which might follow.[19]

A Closer Look at Kabbalism

Before we proceed, we should briefly discuss the relevance of Kabbalism (a system of Jewish mysticism) and its numerology. The Kabbalah holds that every detail in the Torah has mystical significance. Its major texts are the Sefer Yezarah or the Book of Creation, written sometime between the third and sixth centuries A.D., and the Sefer HaZohar or the Book of Splendor, probably written in the thirteenth century A.D. and commonly known in occult circles as the Zohar. Four systems of biblical exegesis dominate Kabbalistic interpretation of the Bible. Notarikon takes the letters of words to form new words by using acrostics; Gematria interprets a word based upon the numerical value of its letters; Timurah substitutes one letter for another; and Tziruf involves the transposing of letters. Another method, Atbah (related to Timurah), involves the permutation of letters, where the first letter of the Hebrew alphabet is replaced by the last, the second letter is replaced by the second-to-the-last, and so on.

With these systems of interpretation, it's possible for Kabbalism to create innumerable meanings and hidden relationships between various words in the Bible. Apparently Kabbalism had a definite influence on the church during the Middle Ages: "The [K]abbala reflects what can be considered as normative exegesis in the Middle Ages both in Jewish and Christian circles. Both were influenced by Gnosticism and Pythagorean numerology and approached scripture allegorically. Mystical numerology occupied the attention of scholars during the days of Luther and was employed as an apologetic just as it was in the days of the Church Fathers."[20]

We will later return to our discussion of the relevance of Kabbalism to the Bible code. For now, we have to wonder: Does the popularity of the Bible code prevision a return to the symbolic and/or mystical allegorization of Scriptures found in the Church Fathers and the Middle Ages? Only time will tell.

The Controversy Continues

Clearly, in its symbolic and mystical applications, controversy had surrounded the subject of Bible numerology since its inception. The current climate certainly won't change matters. As Matt Lauer stated on NBC's "Today" television program after an interview with Drosnin, "Believers and non-believers will debate this for years to come."[21]

Drosnin, for one, however, claims to have carefully done his research:

> I've spent five years checking out the facts. Nothing is taken on faith. I have confirmed every discovery in the Bible code on my own computer, using two different programs—the same one used by the Israeli mathematician [Rips] who first found the code, and the second program written independently of him. I also interviewed the scientists in the United States and Israel who investigated the code.[22]

Whatever one may think of the initial research that inspired Drosnin to write his book, it is evident that there are serious problems with Drosnin's own work. In fact, three of the very people who initially "broke" or confirmed the code have, to varying degrees, publicly disavowed Drosnin's text. In particular they are concerned with its overall lack of scientific methodology and its attempts to predict the future.

Of course, if this phenomenon is genuine, then Drosnin is to be commended for being the first to bring such a startling new discovery to the public's attention. And to be fair, Drosnin emphasizes that his book is only the first report, not the last word, and that there is a great deal we do not yet know about the code.[23] Yet, his book still raises serious questions. In part, that is why those with the most authoritative knowledge in this area have responded negatively to his bestseller.

The June 4, 1997 issue of *USA Today* cited Harold Gans as stating, "Most of Drosnin's claims are unreliable" and, "I can tell you that mathematically, the likelihood of your being able to find something like the 'code will save' or 'Rabin' is very high. You can find 'Drosnin is the Messiah,' and many other things, some of which will be correct and many of which will not be correct. Looking for four or five key words makes no sense. You cannot develop a meaningful statistic on it."[24]

In a public statement Gans released on the internet, he expressed additional concerns:

> The book states that the codes in the Torah can be used to predict future events. This is absolutely unfounded. There is no scientific or mathematical basis for such a statement, and the reason he used to come to such a conclusion in the book is logically flawed. While it is true that some historical events have been shown to be encoded in the Book of Genesis in certain configurations, it is absolutely not true that every similar configuration of "coded" words represents a potential historical event. In fact, quite the opposite is true: most such configurations will be quite random and are expected to occur in any text of sufficient length.[25]

Doron Witztum also publicly declared his displeasure with Drosnin's text:

> Mr. Drosnin's work employs no scientific methodology. No distinction is made between statistically valid codes and accidental appearances, which can be found in any book. For example Drosnin's "code" of the comet Shoemaker-Levy crashing into Jupiter is statistically meaningless. Such a code can be found by accident in one out of any three books checked! [i.e., of equal length to the Pentateuch]. . . . [Concerning predicting the future] Mr. Drosnin's book is based on a false claim. It is impossible to use Torah codes to

predict the future. I myself, as the original researcher of the phenomenon of Torah codes, investigated thoroughly the question of predicting the future. I reached the conclusion that it is impossible. I saw this through experimentation and also a simple point of logic. There are several reasons why it's impossible. I will give the most basic reason. In general, we always have difficulty understanding a text where we don't have any syntax punctuation. In the plain Hebrew text of the Torah, without punctuation, I could easily read the Ten Commandments as telling me to steal and murder. There's a verse that describes Moses being commanded to bring incense. I could easily read it as a commandment to use drugs. All we have is a few isolated encoded words of a hidden text. Maybe we're missing some very critical words. It's literally impossible to learn a coherent story out of the juxtaposition of a few words that may be somehow related. Additionally, just like there is a code that Rabin would be assassinated, I also found a code saying that Churchill would be assassinated. . . . It is therefore unwise, and one could say irresponsible, to make "predictions" based on ELSs of words appearing near each other.[26]

Finally, Elihayu Rips claims, "I do not support Mr. Drosnin's work on the codes nor the conclusion he derives," and "the book is on extremely shaky ground."[27] Rips also said in a press release on June 4, 1997, "All attempts to extract [e.g. personal] messages from Torah codes or to make predictions based on them are futile and of no value."[28]

Other individuals involved in different ways in the codes research, as well as numerous skeptics, have made similar or even more critical statements about Drosnin's work. Daniel Block, professor of Old Testament at Southern Baptist Theological Seminary says, "He takes the Bible and makes it like the Delphic Oracle . . . ambiguous, able to tell you anything you are looking for."[29] Rabbi Daniel Mechanic, a senior international codes lecturer and researcher for the Aish HaTorah Discovery Seminar, alleges that Drosnin's book is statistically invalid and has "no interpretive power."[30] Ronald S. Hendel, who holds a Ph.D. from Harvard University, and is a Hebrew book review editor for *Bible Review*, writes that Drosnin's book is "a journalistic hoax."[31] Shlomo Sternberg, an academic mathematician, a member of the National Academy of Sciences, an orthodox rabbi who has taught the Talmud and rabbinical law for 45 years (besides publishing 14 books, including *Group Theory and Physics*, Cambridge University Press, 1994), and who holds the George Putnam Chair in Pure and Applied Mathematics at Harvard University, calls Drosnin's book and the code phenomenon generally "complete rubbish" and "embarrassing numerological hogwash."[32]

Apparently, however, Elihayu Rips does not discredit Drosnin's work entirely, commenting that it "does have some examples of codes that are statistically significant." The obvious problem, as he points out, is that the vast majority of people reading his book have no basis for distinguishing what, according to serious codes research, is legitimate, and what is not.[33]

While the authors of the original research seem to be happy over the great exposure the codes have received as a result of Drosnin's book, they are also extremely concerned that legitimate code research will be discredited by the overabundance of popular material on the market which contain generally unscientific approaches to the subject. Witztum declared in his public statement:

> We have a very important and valuable phenomenon that has been discovered. It's a scientific discovery that can really help us get a better understanding of the nature of our existence. Rather than have it watered down with people's personal exploitation or misunderstanding, we should be investing more in

serious research and understanding of the phenomenon. . . . by publicizing books and works of examples of codes that have no scientific basis . . . [this]
ruins the integrity of serious research.[34]

So far, we can see that serious research has been done
that seems to indicate the existence of a code in the Bible. But
we also have plenty of skeptics and critics. In our subsequent
chapters, we will take a closer look at this phenomenon and
seek to "decode the Bible code."

4

Hidden Codes: Only in the Bible?

In Drosnin's book *The Bible Code* and other sources, we are told that a genuine code can be found only in the Bible, and not in any other literature. Drosnin claims, "In experiment after experiment, the crossword puzzles [that is, codes] were found only in the Bible, not in *War and Peace*, not in any other book and not in ten million computer-generated cases."[1] To help relieve his initial skepticism, Drosnin asked Rips "if it were not possible to find some similar information in any text, random letter combinations that had no actual meaning."[2] Rips' response was, "Of course you can find random letter combinations in any text. Of course you will find 'Saddam Hussein' in any large enough data base, but you won't find 'Scuds,' 'Russian Missiles,' and the day the war began all at the same place in advance. It doesn't matter if we're looking at a text of 100,000 or 100,000,000 letters, you will not find coherent information—except in the Bible."[3]

In the footnote section of his book, Drosnin discusses an experiment he did on his own:

> I performed my own, more limited, experiment checking 20 Bible code findings displayed in this book, to see if any of the same encodings also appeared in a controlled text of the same size, the first

304,805 letters from the Hebrew translation of *Crime and Punishment*. Half of the names and phrases did not appear at all, and none appeared with coherent related information.[4]

Thus, although "President Kennedy" appeared in *Crime and Punishment*, the words "to die" and "Dallas" were not encoded in the same place. "Shakespeare" appeared once, but was not encoded with "Hamlet" or "Macbeth."[5] "The [code confirming] pattern was consistent for all twenty names and phrases checked."[6]

Searching Elsewhere for Codes

Drosnin's Assertion

Drosnin says he never found the kind of coherent information in *Crime and Punishment* that he found in the Bible. He cited Rips as saying that:

> . . . only in the Bible code is there consistent, coherent information [revealed]. And no one has found in *War and Peace* or *Crime and Punishment* the accurate prediction of an assassination a year before it happened, or the correct date of a war three weeks in advance. No one has found anything like that in any other book, in any translation, or in any original Hebrew text except the Bible.[7]

Drosnin even claims that he and Rips could read the Bible code like the daily newspaper:

> We found . . . one thousand world events encoded in the Bible. It was possible on any given day to pick up the *New York Times*, the *Jerusalem Post*, and if the story on the front page was important enough, to find it encoded in a document that had been written 3000 years ago. The information, time after time, proved as accurate as the current newspaper accounts, the names, the places, the dates, all encoded in Genesis

through Deuteronomy. And sometimes it was found in advance. Six months before the 1992 election, the code revealed Bill Clinton's victory. Connected to "Clinton" was his future title "president."[8]

Drosnin, Rips, and others agree that it's possible for some names or events to appear by chance in other literature. However, they argue that only in the Bible do we find a great deal of information that, from a statistical standpoint, could not possibly have happened by chance.

Refuting Drosnin's Claim

How have critics responded to that assertion? By saying that the results actually *aren't* impossible. Peter Coy, writing in the June 16, 1997 issue of *Business Week,* cites Andrew W. Lo, a Massachusetts Institute of Technology professor of finance who observes, "Given enough time, enough attempts and enough imagination, almost any pattern can be teased out of any data set."[9] The June 19, 1997 issue of *Newsweek* says that numerous mathematicians and code breakers "are treating it as a statistician's version of cold fusion." The article cites Harvard University mathematician Shlomo Sternberg, who warns, "You can become clever at manipulating a text, making something appear that looks miraculous."[10] And Don Foster of Vassar College, a professor who analyzes Shakespearean texts with computers, comments, "A wicked little devil is whispering in my ear that these [code finders] could do the same with a telephone directory if they thought it was a spiritually significant text."[11]

If it took Rips, Drosnin, and others years of research to come up with the messages they have found in the Bible, then perhaps they just have not looked hard enough or long enough or discovered a method for finding similar messages in *Crime and Punishment, War and Peace,* or other texts of similar length. D. Trull, editor of *Enigma* magazine, writes, "If you have a text of sufficient length and get to choose your method of rearranging it, you can discover just about any 'encrypted message' you can imagine."[12]

Drosnin himself seems to have proven that to be the case. He made this challenge to his critics: "When my critics find a message about the assassination of a Prime Minister encrypted in *Moby Dick*, I will believe them."[13] Brendan McKay took up the challenge and searched through *Moby Dick*, and in fact, found a message about such an assassination. Actually, he found 13 predicted assassinations of public figures, several being Prime Ministers or their equivalents.[14] The death of President Anastasio Samoza was accurately "predicted" with the mention of the date of his assassination on September 21, 1956, along with five closely spaced sequences that said "pres," "Samoza," "dies," "hewasshot," and "gun."[15]

Brendan McKay also conducted a search of *Law of the Sea Treaty* and found encoded within the text "Hear the law of the sea," and "safe U.N. ocean convention to enclose tuna."[16] More significantly, at odds of a quadrillion to one against it, McKay examined a Hebrew translation of *War and Peace* and found in skip code 59 different words related to *Chanukah*, including "Maccabees" and "miracle of lights."[17]

In the December 1997 issue of *Skeptical Inquirer*, physicist David E. Thomas pointed out that, searching forward only with a list of 25 names, he has found thousands of hidden occurrences and many complex messages in the English King James translation of Genesis, and in a well-known court case, Edwards vs. Aguillard, we have this: "I was able to easily produce complex hidden messages in all the texts I worked with." His study, all done with non-Hebrew literature, reveals examples equally spectacular as those in Drosnin's book. For example, in the King James Version of Genesis, he found 5,812 hidden "UFOs" with dozens hovering close to or flying through the hidden word "Roswell." He noted, "As the puzzle step is changed, linked matches appear and disappear with astonishing frequency," and "codes can be engineered—*made* to happen. You just have to know how to harvest the field of possibilities." He further stated, "Brendan McKay (in personal communication) showed me how to find hidden words much more efficiently, and a search of the King James Version of Genesis at all possible steps for my list of 25 names came up with over one million additional matches."

Thomas also shows that Drosnin's probability arguments are flawed and that, "Once I learned how to navigate in puzzle space, finding 'incredible' predictions became a routine affair." He found, for example, "Trinity," "Los Alamos," "atom," and "bomb" coded together in the very same section containing references to "security," "test," and "anti-fascist."

The Need for More Research

In their initial searches, then, critics have come up with codes that reveal "consistent coherent information" in non-biblical texts. However, the *extent* and significance of data found by Rips and other Bible code researchers does not yet seem to be duplicated in a nonbiblical text. So we can only ask: Will the initial research of these nonbiblical texts stand final critical review? Will critics who spend a similar amount of time "code researching" other texts find code patterns equally startling to those that Witztum and others found in the Bible? If they do, then they will have shown that there is merit in the argument that a text of sufficient length could be manipulated in ways that will produce "miraculous" encrypted messages.

Witztum, Rips, Satinover, and Drosnin point out that no one has yet submitted a rebuttal to the initial *Statistical Science* paper (although some are working on it) and they remind critics that the key scientists who examined the Bible code have confirmed its technical aspects. This includes the three referees for *Statistical Science;* Harold Gans, the retired expert code analyst; and the professors at Harvard, Yale, and Hebrew Universities—all eight of whom started out as skeptics and ended up becoming believers. Professors H. Furstenberg of

Hebrew University, I. Piateski-Shapiro of Yale University, D. Kazhdan of Harvard University, and J. Bernstein also of Harvard have all stated that the code is real. Yet they also point out that the interpretation of the phenomenon is still open to question, and that more research is needed.[18]

To be fair, in his book, Dr. Satinover discusses some of the common criticisms and misunderstandings relating to the codes and provides brief responses. First, he points out that although anyone would be able to find words at equidistant intervals, the nature of the Bible code phenomenon lies in an entirely different category. The Bible code contains systematic or rule-determined sets of related equidistant letter sequences at *minimal* equidistant intervals in such significant quantities that it is very unlikely they would have occurred by chance.

Second, he points out that the freedom to choose skips does not make it easier to find whatever one wants because the skips *"must be minimal* (or near minimal) *intervals for that word."*[19]

Third, he also shows why some words that aren't at their minimal equidistant interval do not provide opportunity for random occurrences to appear meaningful when they really aren't.

Fourth, the argument that just about anything can be seen as being "related" is irrelevant because the data used by the principals was on "historical fact subject to no interpretation."[20]

Fifth, he shows that a statistical effect based on the structure of Hebrew cannot account for the results and that a few dating mistakes in the original data itself present no problem. After such mistakes were corrected, the results actually improved.[21] Satinover concludes that "careful scientific scrutiny of the codes leaves this as the one likely unhidden flaw: the possibility that the data set was in some way inadvertently skewed."[22]

While these are legitimate responses to some issues, we will still have to see how other critics reply to them. Further, an inadvertent skewing of the data is not the only conceivable code disproof; again we will have to wait and see. But the responses do not deal with larger concerns relative to the Bible code, nor do they deal with other problems relative to methodology and the "nature" of the code itself, which will be discussed later.

The reason we remain cautious is because on more than one occasion seemingly *very* solid scientific research has been published, only to have flaws invalidate the entire research some years down the road. Satinover himself asked Professor Kass about the basic attitude that a typical statistician would probably have toward the Bible code, and Dr. Kass responded:

> We see a very large number of experiments with seemingly solid claims that turn out not to be true. This happens most typically in clinical trials of various new medications, or other medical treatments. Most of them achieve statistical significance at first, and they're published—that is how they come to our attention—but then after increasingly regular scrutiny over a long period of time, they eventually fail. So we're accustomed to taking initial trials with a grain of salt, no matter how successful they are—especially ones with highly unexpected results.[23]

Kass also stated, "It's a good puzzle and the [*Statistical Science*] paper had no glaringly obvious problems, but nobody considered for a moment that the results might be valid. None of the referees changed their minds in the course of the review. It has been my hope that someone would rise to the occasion and definitively solve the mystery."[24]

The truth is that some of the most able researchers in the entire world are now attempting to do just this. They are joining forces and looking into the code, due, in part, no doubt, to the monumental implications should the code prove true. Indeed, Satinover points out:

> As I write, a semisecret project examining the codes is under way at one of the world's major academic

centers. Involved in it are some of the world's most eminent names in mathematics, computer sciences and statistics. Most of the participants in this project are skeptics grown irritated, some even angry at the worldwide and rapidly growing interest the codes are attracting. Their aim is once and for all to lay such absurd propositions to rest by demonstrating a flaw at the heart of the research.[25]

Later in his book, Satinover said:

At present, a number of world-class statisticians from universities around the world have combined their efforts, to find the fatal flaw they are certain must be there—Harvard, Cornell, the Princeton Institute for Advanced Study, Australian National University (ANU), and universities in Israel are among the institutions represented by this group.[26]

Even Dr. Satinover agrees that some of the criticism against the Bible code "is quite sophisticated—at the very edge of mathematical statistics' power—and needs to be taken seriously."[27]

Like many people, Satinover wants to believe the codes are real. But he realizes that the proof is simply not yet there: "To be fair, I myself can't be 100 percent certain of the results. I admit that I *want* the codes to be what they seem to be. I happen to want there to be a God, because I am not at all sanguine about the alternative."[28] Who would be? But again, even if the code were valid, even *then* it wouldn't prove the existence of God to skeptics for whom no proof is adequate. And Christian theologians argue that the evidences for God are already sufficiently persuasive that "proof by code" is, for all practical purposes, unnecessary.[29] In other words, the code isn't needed to prove God's existence. God has already taken care of that, they say, according to Romans 1:19-21: "What may be known about God is plain to them, because God has made it plain to them. For since the creation of the world

God's invisible qualities—his eternal power and divine nature—have been clearly seen, being understood from what has been made, so that men are without excuse."

People who desperately want the code to be true to prove God's existence are looking in the wrong place and placing their faith in the wrong object. As Satinover warns:

> We do not know yet whether the phenomenon will continue to resist refutation, or will prove itself yet another in a long line of insubstantial religious enthusiasms. . . . Perhaps the Bible code will prove to be yet another chimera—vastly more sophisticated and befuddling, more perhaps than anything that has come before.

And . . .

> The need for swift, serious scrutiny arose directly out of the stunning impact the codes had already had in people's lives. It would be a tragedy if such an effect were based on something false: First because false belief always breeds tragedy; second, the disillusionment that would follow.[30]

There is yet another question that we must raise: Why would it be necessary for God to encode the Torah in such a way as to prove its divine authorship through the discovery of unimpeachable future knowledge—down to the *smallest* detail? If it were true that, according to the Gaon of Vilna, "all of existence was written in the Torah,"[31] why would that *degree* of detail be needed? All of existence encompasses an awful lot—including an awful lot of the evil humanity has accomplished over the millennia. Doesn't it seem a bit unusual for the Torah to encode this extent of detail when something much less would suffice? And, Christian theologians ask, if God's Word is eternal as Scripture declares (Psalm 119:89, Isaiah 40:8, 1 Peter 1:25), why would a holy and righteous God encode His Word with the accounts of *all* human evil throughout *all* time?

5

Interpreting the Code: Some Key Dilemmas

Is the Bible code a superior revelation to what we have in the plain text of the Bible?

Apparently Drosnin believes so. He says the Bible code is "a Bible beneath the Bible."[1] For Drosnin the most important message in the Bible is not that which is found in the plain text, but the coded information hidden within the text. He says, "Now it [the Bible] can be read as it was always intended to be read."[2] If it's true that the Bible was always intended to be read in coded form (which could not happen until the advent of computers), then, critics charge, God seems to have made a rather significant mistake in allowing the Bible to be written two to three thousand years before computers were invented.

Drosnin further argues, "We always thought of the Bible as a book. We now know that was only its first incarnation. It is also a computer program . . . something that its original author actually designed to be interactive and ever changing."[3] Yet does it seem plausible that the Bible code could be ever-changing, when the message of the Bible itself is one that has never changed? If the Bible's secret meaning is fluid, what are the implications for its surface meaning, which is said to be unchanging?

The Plain Text vs. the Hidden

The plain message of the Bible includes many prophecies about the future that God Himself says will *definitely* be fulfilled (Deuteronomy 18:21-22; Isaiah 48:3-7; Jeremiah 28:9). What, then, do we do when we find that a message encoded in the Bible tells us that predicted events are only *possibilities* and can be prevented?

Drosnin says, "Each predicted event appears to be encoded with *at least two possible outcomes*."[4] But what happens to biblical prophecy (which has unavoidable outcomes) if every Bible code prophecy has two outcomes? Why would the God of the Bible give one outcome in the plain text (which He says will be fulfilled), and two possible outcomes in the hidden text? Further, Drosnin says the Bible code contains "all our possible futures"—which, it would seem, could be endless. How, then, do we find the one true future?

Thus Drosnin writes, "No one knows if what is encoded in the Bible is predetermined or is only a possibility. My own guess is that the Bible encodes all our possible futures and what we do determines the outcome."[5] Drosnin's guess creates a dilemma, for it contradicts the plain text of the Bible, which states that God has preordained all of what happens in our world, and that He is in full control of the future (*see* Isaiah 14:24,27).

In the matter of future possibilities, Satinover agrees with Drosnin:

> The codes do not present a portrait of a fixedly predetermined world, though upon first consideration they may seem to. They show, rather, the crucial role of a genuinely free human agency in determining—precisely *in participating in* determining—what *actually* happens in history from among the options laid down by divine providence.[6]

Both Drosnin and Satinover discuss how the paradoxical findings of quantum mechanics relate to the Bible code. For example, in particle physics, the indeterminacy of the position of an electron is paralleled to the indeterminacy of the Bible code as it relates, for example, to multiple predictions or other "fuzzy" aspects of the code. Thus, for example:

> Quantum mechanics does not merely say that *we don't yet know what causes the actual outcome* [of electron states]. Nor does it say that *we can never know even though there is some such determining influence.* It says, rather, *that there is absolutely nothing causing the actual events*—more precisely, *nothing in the physical universe.*[7]

This field certainly is paradoxical—and controversial—and there are a lot of common misconceptions concerning quantum mechanics especially as it is interpreted in New Age applications. (Dr. Weldon discussed some of this in his *Encyclopedia of New Age Beliefs* [Eugene, OR: Harvest House Publishers, 1996]).

Given the influence of such things as Kabbalism and the parallels to indeterminate quantum mechanical phenomena in the Bible code, we have to ask the logical questions, How "stable" is such a "code"? and, Could the "theology" of the Bible code be the "theology" of the Bible? A "theology" that is parallel to or influenced by quantum mechanical considerations is certainly not going to remain a historical biblical theology.

The inherent difficulties of divine sovereignty and human freedom/responsibility aside, there does seem to be a tendency in the promoters of the Bible code to interpret God in ways that are either not biblical or quasi-biblical. Satinover, for example, states that the Bible code has certain inherent features or characteristics that sets it apart from common theological assumptions and aligns it more to the mystical connections of Kabbalism:

One of the striking features of the Bible code is that it presents a picture of "chance" and predestination that is eerily parallel to what has emerged in quantum mechanics. These ideas are completely at odds with the mechanistic presumptions of the Enlightenment, yet they are not identical to common theological assumptions either. They have *striking similarity*, however, to certain conceptions found in the ancient Jewish tradition, especially in its less familiar, more "mystical" kabbalistic dimensions.[8]

Thus, the Bible code seems to imply that the biblical God is no longer sovereign or omnipotent—at least not all the time—and that He may restrict His sovereignty and omnipotence to allow for our freedom.[9]

Biblically, while the interrelationship between divine sovereignty and human responsibility is a mystery, we clearly see both present in the Bible. We see no evidence that a God who is sovereign must restrict or "withdraw" His divine attributes in order to allow for man's freedom. Biblically, God is simply the sovereign Lord who does as He pleases and who is sovereign in and over all things at all times.

It is the parallels between quantum mechanics and the Bible code that causes Satinover to conclude, "God lays out the broad pattern of history, acts in the world alongside us, [but willingly] 'contracts' some portions of His omnipotence so that we may be granted the gift of genuine freedom."[10] However, nowhere in the plain text of Scripture do we see anything that indicates God "contracts" part of His omnipotence—or His sovereignty—in such a manner.

So the questions becomes this: If the Bible code "requires" a reformulation of the nature of God along the lines of quantum mechanical and kabbalistic thought, what kind of God will we end up with? (Chapter 9 offers more on this.)

Mention of the Code in the Bible?

Drosnin argues that the Bible code is the divinely sealed revelation spoken of in the biblical books of Daniel, Isaiah, and Revelation.[11] But for a variety of reasons, this is untenable. Drosnin quotes Isaiah 29:11: "For you this salvation ['vision' in the NIV, or New International Version] is nothing but words sealed in a book." It is the first reference to the secret "sealed book" in the Bible. [12] However, this Bible passage has nothing to do with a coded sealed book, as Drosnin claims. In Isaiah 29, God is warning Jerusalem of impending judgment for her spiritual hardness of heart and idolatries. The Hebrew word rendered "salvation" in the King James Version (KJV) is correctly translated "vision." It refers to the vision God had given Isaiah. It is this vision of impending doom that is hidden to the inhabitants of Jerusalem because of their spiritual poverty. Because they cannot understand their condition or comprehend their fate, the vision is *like* "words sealed in a scroll." God's judgment is imminent, yet they are blinded to it.

It is one thing to say that God's vision is like a sealed book that people are unable to understand because of the hardness of their hearts. It is entirely another thing to interpret this verse as teaching that there is a secret code in the Bible. Drosnin is wrong. Read what he writes next, citing Isaiah 29:11-12,18:

> At first, states Isaiah, no one would be able to open the "sealed" book. "And if you give the book to someone who can read, and say to him, 'Read this please,' he will answer, 'I can't, it is sealed.'" But finally Isaiah predicts the "sealed book" will be opened: "On that day the deaf will hear the words of the book and from the gloom and the darkness the eyes of the blind will see it."[13]

This is an incorrect interpretation of Isaiah. The phrase "on that day" refers to the future millennial age, not a computer-generated Bible code of today. Any standard Bible commentary will reveal this. Isaiah is predicting that the spiritually deaf and blind will one day understand God's truth and holiness.

Nevertheless, Drosnin goes on to argue that the book of Isaiah actually reveals that the "sealed book" is the "Bible code." "And in the hidden text, [that is, a different code revealed by using slightly different word breaks between existing letters to form new words] the same verses of Isaiah reveal that the sealed book is the Bible code. 'He recognized the words, they will be computerized, his report they heard on this day, the secrets, the magical words of the book.'"[14] This is just more unfounded speculation.

To further argue that the information sealed in the book of Daniel (12:4) and Revelation (5:5) is this same Bible code is also unfounded.

Interpreting the Bible

Consider an illustration of how biblical numerology can be used to misinterpret the Bible. In the Kabbalistic gematria, we find a system of biblical numerology that supplies hidden meanings to the actual words of the Bible, based on the letters' numerical value. *The Harper Collins Bible Dictionary* supplies the following example. Even though Genesis 14:14 declares that Abraham took 318 men on a military mission the numerological "truth" is that he took only one—his servant Eliezer. Why? Because the name Eliezer has a numerical value of 318.[15] In a similar fashion, because the phrase *yb'sylh* in Genesis 49:10 had a numerical value of 358, it was believed on those grounds alone that the passage was Messianic since the Hebrew word for Messiah also has a numerical value of 358.[16]

The hermeneutical system of the Kabbalists was and is clearly subjective and mystical. It involves a reinterpretation of the plain meaning of the biblical text, indeed, endless

reinterpretations: "The various possibilities of symbolic interpretation changed the scriptures into an 'open text' pregnant
with infinite meanings."[17] Any system that has so many different methods of interpreting the Bible and involves multiple
"interpenetrating meanings," "encryptions," and mysterious
hidden meanings is certainly not going to help us understand
the true intent of the Author of Scripture.[18]

One illustration of this is found in the Kabbalistic misinterpretation of the biblical creation account. Kabbalists use the
Torah as a "map" of existence through space and time,
standing, like a deity, outside of it and above it. The physical
world is seen as a creation of the Torah and in particular the
letters of the Torah, which are God's agency for creation. Satinover cites the Zohar, "When the Holy One . . . created the
world, He did so by means of the secret power of letters" and,
"When the Holy One . . . created the world, He created it by
means of letters of the Torah, all the letters of the alphabet
having presented themselves before Him until finally the
letter Beth was chosen for the starting point. Moreover, *the various combinations of the letters and all their permutations* presented themselves to participate in the Creation."[19]

The only problem is that letters don't have secret powers,
nor does God in His omnipotence require letters to create
the universe. This is the problem with mysticism; you end up
with all sorts of speculation, the value of which is rarely sub-
stantiated. Even Satinover ends up interpreting John 1:1, a
clear reference to Jesus' deity *(see* John 1:14) as an apparent
reference to the Torah: "all things were made by it (King James
Version: Him); and without it was not anything made that was
made." The "it" clearly refers to Jesus Christ; however, Satinover has "it" referring to the Torah in an alleged confirmation of Kabbalistic teaching.[20]

Satinover also points out that the accounts of the Jewish
mystics "depart radically" from the literal understanding of the
creation of the world. Thus, "Jewish sages have long maintained

that only children and others capable of no more than simple understanding should be encouraged to read the account of the creation in Genesis with absolute literalism: six 24-hour days, and so on." He adds, "Genesis in short, is not simply *a description*, it is the very instrument of the act of creation itself, a blueprint in the Mind of God made manifest in physical form."[21] Thus God did not literally create Adam and Eve from the dust of the earth, as the Bible teaches.[22] This is a misinterpretation, according to Kabbalistic "understanding."

Clearly, the problem with all this is that the Bible can be made to teach anything and everything the mystics want it to. Through their interpretations, the Bible ends up teaching nothing because nothing it teaches has any binding authority outside the mind of a mystic *(see* chapter 9).

Still Learning Hebrew?

Another area of concern is that Drosnin is not always careful with the Hebrew text that he translates. To be fair, as he claims, he had to learn it by himself, from scratch. But he also claims he had his translations checked by experts. "The translations of all encodings have been confirmed by the authoritative R. Alcalay Hebrew-English dictionary (Massada, 1990) and the standard unabridged Hebrew dictionary by A. Even-Shashon (Kiryat Sefer, 1985). And all the Bible code material quoted in this book has been checked by Israeli translators, who worked with me during the entire five-year investigation."[23]

Yet what about Drosnin's mistranslation of Isaiah 41:23? In this verse, God mocks the powerless gods of the pagans, saying, "Tell us what the future holds so that we may know you are gods." But Drosnin mistranslates this as saying, "To see the future you must look backwards."[24] Drosnin further claims, erroneously, that the name the Egyptian pharaoh gave Joseph, Zaphenath-Paneah, "has a very clear meaning in Hebrew" and actually means "decoder of the code." "So the

Bible calls Joseph 'decoder of the code,'"[25] says Drosnin. "Perhaps no one has seen it before, because no one knew there was a code in the Bible."[26] Drosnin also supplies an "alternate" translation for this Egyptian name: "Joseph encoded, you will decode." Then Drosnin points out the obvious: "But Joseph cannot be the encoder"—because the Torah didn't even exist at the time of Joseph. God gave the Torah to Moses 350 years later.

Next we find out that Joseph's name in Hebrew means "it will be added" and that "the full hidden text in Genesis 41:45 reads, 'the code will be added, you will decode it.'"[27] All of this is unfounded speculation.

Drosnin also tells us the code "suggests that even the writing of the Laws on the stone tablets may have been computer-generated!"[28] After citing Exodus 32:16, he says that encoded in the same verse is a hidden message, "it was made by computer."[29] Here we have another example of Drosnin's "code" contradicting the plain meaning of the text. The text clearly declares that the tablets were written by the finger of God (31:18). We don't know exactly how they were written, but certainly God did not sit down at a computer.

Clearly, a code that can so easily be used to mistranslate or reinterpret the plain statements of the Bible would seem pointless. Because the matter of translation and interpretation is so crucial to Drosnin's conclusions, let's consider the following observations on Hebrew and other matters from Drs. Clifford and Barbara Wilson.

Reading into the Text?

In the case of the death of Israel's Prime Minister Rabin, the preset computer was asked to find his name, and it soon did. In all the multiplicity of possible combinations, the name appeared only once, picked out by "a skip sequence" of 4,772 letters. On the matrix, the name is spelled out vertically.

When we transliterate the letters of Rabin's name into English, they look like this:

Y

Ts

H

K

R

B

I

N

A few points should be made in colloquial English so that we can understand what's happening here. First, the letters of the word under scrutiny will be equidistant from each other. They can read up or down, or they can read in order from the left side to the right side, or from the right side to the left side (which is how Hebrew is normally written), or they can even read diagonally, in any direction or angle. The key factor is that the letters must be equidistant.

Drosnin points out that at the same place we find Rabin's name we also find the name of Rabin's assassin: "Amir." It is above the name of Yitzhak Rabin. Nearby we also find the name of the place (Tel Aviv) where the murder would take place, and even the year in which it was to occur. It is given as 5756 according to the Jewish calendar, this being 1995–1996 in "Western" terms. (The Jewish year starts in September.)

Michael Drosnin's summary is stated clearly:

> "Amir" was encoded in the same places as "Yitzhak Rabin" and "assassin who will assassinate." Moreover, the words "name of the assassin" appeared in the plain text of the Bible in the same verse that the name "Amir" appeared in the hidden text. And also, in that same verse, the hidden text stated, "he struck, he killed the Prime Minister."

He was even identified as an Israeli who shot at close range, "His killer: one of his people, the one who got close."

The code revealed when and where it would happen. "In 5756," the Hebrew year that began in September 1995, crossed both "Tel Aviv" and "Rabin assassination." "Amir" appeared in the same place.[30]

It all sounds very convincing, and in fact we do not deny that some of it is beyond comprehension in regard to the details given. The problem is that this alleged prophecy involves more of what is called *eisogesis* (reading into the text) as opposed to *exegesis* (explaining the truth from the meaning of the text itself).

Shlomo Sternberg makes a good point about "the assassin who will assassinate." He writes,

The horizontal phrase marked by Drosnin (p.16 —Ed.) in squares means "a slayer who happens to have killed." Drosnin mistranslates these three words as "assassin that will assassinate." With this method, it is pretty clear that you can predict anything.[31]

Independently of Dr. Sternberg, we had already checked this out in our Hebrew Bible. The relevant passage about "assassinate" turns out to be instructions to the ancient Hebrews about a person who *unintentionally* kills another person and needs to flee to an established "City of Refuge" for protection. This is how the passage reads in the Authorized Version of the Bible, relating to three of the cities of refuge on Israel's side of the Jordan River.

That the slayer might flee thither, which should kill his neighbor unawares, and hated him not in times past; and that fleeing to one of these cities he might live (Deuteronomy 4:42).

It surely is a distortion to suggest that this can be translated as "assassin will assassinate." Such interpretations according to preconceived notions can considerably reduce our confidence in Drosnin's conclusions here and at other places. In fact, by such wrong interpretation, Drosnin throws doubt on the credibility of his thesis when it comes to his personal transliteration, translation, interpretation, and application of the Hebrew text.

We have included on pages 68–70 three excerpts of Hebrew text. The first (Chart 1) is from Drosnin's book *The Bible Code*, supposedly showing where the Bible itself has the phrase, "assassin will assassinate."

○   YITZHAK RABIN   □   ASSASSIN WILL ASSASSINATE

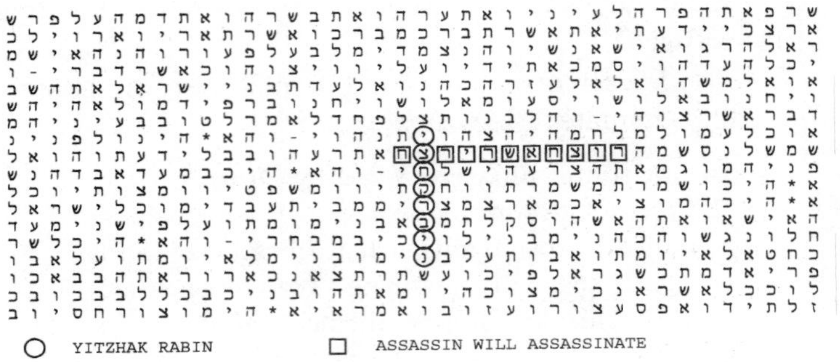

CHART 1

The second excerpt is from the British and Foreign Bible Society translation of the Hebrew Old Testament. It comes from Deuteronomy 4:42, and is marked Chart 2.

The third excerpt is from the *Interlinear Old Testament* published by Baker Book House, and it is marked Chart 3. The interlinear translation is "the manslayer . . . who killed," which appears in the middle of a sentence. In fact, Drosnin takes part of the previous word (remember, Hebrew is read from right to left), *shamah*, which means simply "there," and then adds the final letter (equivalent to the English "h") so that he will have a new meaning, which he gives as "name of the assassin who will assassinate."

29 יִשְׁמְעוֹן וְלֹא יֹאכְלוּן וְלֹא יְרִיחֻן: וּבִקַּשְׁתֶּם מִשָּׁם אֶת־יְהֹוָה

ל אֱלֹהֶיךָ וּמָצָאתָ כִּי תִדְרְשֶׁנּוּ בְּכָל־לְבָבְךָ וּבְכָל־נַפְשֶׁךָ: בַּצַּר
לְךָ וּמְצָאוּךָ כֹּל הַדְּבָרִים הָאֵלֶּה בְּאַחֲרִית הַיָּמִים וְשַׁבְתָּ

31 עַד־יְהֹוָה אֱלֹהֶיךָ וְשָׁמַעְתָּ בְּקֹלוֹ: כִּי אֵל רַחוּם יְהֹוָה אֱלֹהֶיךָ
לֹא יַרְפְּךָ וְלֹא יַשְׁחִיתֶךָ וְלֹא יִשְׁכַּח אֶת־בְּרִית אֲבֹתֶיךָ אֲשֶׁר

32 נִשְׁבַּע לָהֶם: כִּי שְׁאַל־נָא לְיָמִים רִאשֹׁנִים אֲשֶׁר־הָיוּ לְפָנֶיךָ
לְמִן־הַיּוֹם אֲשֶׁר בָּרָא אֱלֹהִים ׀ אָדָם עַל־הָאָרֶץ וּלְמִקְצֵה
הַשָּׁמַיִם וְעַד־קְצֵה הַשָּׁמָיִם הֲנִהְיָה כַּדָּבָר הַגָּדוֹל הַזֶּה אוֹ

33 הֲנִשְׁמַע כָּמֹהוּ: הֲשָׁמַע עָם קוֹל אֱלֹהִים מְדַבֵּר מִתּוֹךְ־הָאֵשׁ

34 כַּאֲשֶׁר־שָׁמַעְתָּ אַתָּה וַיֶּחִי: אוֹ ׀ הֲנִסָּה אֱלֹהִים לָבוֹא לָקַחַת
לוֹ גוֹי מִקֶּרֶב גּוֹי בְּמַסֹּת בְּאֹתֹת וּבְמוֹפְתִים וּבְמִלְחָמָה וּבְיָד
חֲזָקָה וּבִזְרוֹעַ נְטוּיָה וּבְמוֹרָאִים גְּדֹלִים כְּכֹל אֲשֶׁר־עָשָׂה

לה לָכֶם יְהֹוָה אֱלֹהֵיכֶם בְּמִצְרַיִם לְעֵינֶיךָ: אַתָּה הָרְאֵתָ לָדַעַת

36 כִּי יְהֹוָה הוּא הָאֱלֹהִים אֵין עוֹד מִלְבַדּוֹ: מִן־הַשָּׁמַיִם
הִשְׁמִיעֲךָ אֶת־קֹלוֹ לְיַסְּרֶךָ וְעַל־הָאָרֶץ הֶרְאֲךָ אֶת־אִשּׁוֹ

37 הַגְּדוֹלָה וּדְבָרָיו שָׁמַעְתָּ מִתּוֹךְ הָאֵשׁ: וְתַחַת כִּי אָהַב אֶת־
אֲבֹתֶיךָ וַיִּבְחַר בְּזַרְעוֹ אַחֲרָיו וַיּוֹצִאֲךָ בְּפָנָיו בְּכֹחוֹ הַגָּדֹל

38 מִמִּצְרָיִם: לְהוֹרִישׁ גּוֹיִם גְּדֹלִים וַעֲצֻמִים מִמְּךָ מִפָּנֶיךָ לַהֲבִיאֲךָ

39 לָתֶת־לְךָ אֶת־אַרְצָם נַחֲלָה כַּיּוֹם הַזֶּה: וְיָדַעְתָּ הַיּוֹם וַהֲשֵׁבֹתָ
אֶל־לְבָבֶךָ כִּי יְהֹוָה הוּא הָאֱלֹהִים בַּשָּׁמַיִם מִמַּעַל וְעַל־

מ הָאָרֶץ מִתָּחַת אֵין עוֹד: וְשָׁמַרְתָּ אֶת־חֻקָּיו וְאֶת־מִצְוֹתָיו
אֲשֶׁר אָנֹכִי מְצַוְּךָ הַיּוֹם אֲשֶׁר יִיטַב לְךָ וּלְבָנֶיךָ אַחֲרֶיךָ וּלְמַעַן
תַּאֲרִיךְ יָמִים עַל־הָאֲדָמָה אֲשֶׁר יְהֹוָה אֱלֹהֶיךָ נֹתֵן לְךָ כָּל־
הַיָּמִים:*

פ

41 שְׁלִישׁ אָז יַבְדִּיל מֹשֶׁה שָׁלֹשׁ עָרִים בְּעֵבֶר הַיַּרְדֵּן מִזְרְחָה שָׁמֶשׁ: לָנֻס
42 לָאֹשׁ שָׁמָּה רוֹצֵחַ אֲשֶׁר יִרְצַח אֶת־רֵעֵהוּ בִּבְלִי־דַעַת וְהוּא לֹא־
שֹׂנֵא לוֹ מִתְּמֹל שִׁלְשֹׁם וְנָס אֶל־אַחַת מִן־הֶעָרִים הָאֵל וָחָי:

את־בצר

v. 42. סבירין האלה

CHART 2

and so that you may
prolong *your* days on the
earth, which Jehovah our
God is giving to you all the
days.

⁴¹Then Moses separated
three cities beyond the
Jordan, toward the sun-
rising, ⁴²that the manslayer
might flee there, he who
killed his neighbor un-
awares, and did not hate
him *in* times before, and he
fleeing to one of these
cities might live: ⁴³Bezer
in the wilderness, in the
tableland, for the Reuben-
ites; and Ramoth in Gilead,
for the Gadites; and Golan
in Bashan, for the Manas-
sites.

⁴⁴And this *is* the law
which Moses set before the
sons of Israel; ⁴⁵these are
the testimonies and the
statutes and the ordinances
which Moses spoke to the
sons of Israel when they
came out of Egypt

⁴⁶beyond the Jordan, in the
valley opposite Beth-peor,
in the land of Sihon the king
of the Amorites, who lived
at Heshbon, whom Moses
and the sons of Israel struck
when they came out of
Egypt ⁴⁷And they took
possession of his land, and
the land of Og the king of
Bashan, the two kings of
the Amorites who *were*
beyond the Jordan, toward
the sunrising; ⁴⁸from Aroer,
which *is* on the lip of the
river of Arnon, even to
Mount Sion, which *is*
Hermon; ⁴⁹and all the
Arabah beyond the Jordan
eastward, even to the sea of
the Arabah, under the
slopes of Pisgah.

5414 430	123	3068 834	5921 3117 748	
is God your Jehovah which	the	on (your)	may you so and that	
giving		,earth	days prolong	

the all to
,days you

⁴¹ 8121 4217 3383 5676 5892 7969 4872 1914

,sun toward the beyond cities three Moses separated
rising the Jordan Then

⁴² 7523 8033 5127

,knowing without his killed who the there for
neighbor man-slayer fleeing

5892 259 5127 8032 8543 8130 1961

cities of one to and before times to hating not and
fled he him was

⁴³ 7206 4334 776 4057 1121 2425

the of level the in the in Bezer and these
:Reubenites land ,wilderness :lived

⁴⁴ 2088 4520 1568 7433

And the of in Golan and the of in Ramoth and
(is) this ,Manassites ,Bashan ;Gadites ,Gilead

⁴⁵ 57 43 428 3478 4872 7760 834 8451

the These Israel the before Moses set which law the
testimonies are of sons

5749 1121 4872 1696 834 8451 3478

,Israel the to Moses spoke which the and the and
of sons judgments statutes

⁴⁶ 1047 4136 1516 3383 5676 5927

:peor Beth- opposite the in the valley the beyond from they when
,Jordan ,Egypt out came

2809 3427 834 567 4428 5511 776

whom in was who the the the Sihon the in
,Heshbon living Amorites of king of land

⁴⁷ 3423 4714 5927 3478 4872 5221

took they And from they when ,Israel the and Moses struck
of possession ,Egypt out came of sons

567 4428 1316 5747 776 776

the kings the ,Bashan the Og the and and his
,Amorites of two of king of land ,land

⁴⁸ 5921 6177 769 4217 7865 2022

on which from Aroer ,sun- toward the beyond what
(is) rising the Jordan (were)

⁴⁹ 3605 2268 769 2022 7865 2768

and :Hermon which ,Sion Mount even ,Arnon tor- the the
of rent of edge

⁶¹⁶⁰ ⁸⁴⁷⁸ 6160 3220 5704 4217 3383 5676

under the the even ,eastward the beyond the
,Arabah of sea to Jordan Arabah

6449 798

:Pisgah slopes the
of

CHART 3

Now, the context of the passage relates to someone who inadvertently kills another person and flees to a City of Refuge, where, under certain circumstances, he is safe. This is very different from the application given by Michael Drosnin, which has to do with an assassin who deliberately murdered Israel's Prime Minister Rabin. At best it is a mistranslation. It is also an example of *eisogesis*—reading something into the text. Either way, we have before us a serious misrepresentation of what the text really is saying.

Selective Transliteration
The Tokyo Gas Attack

On March 20, 1995, there was a horrific terrorist attack in the city of Tokyo, which was the work of an extremist religious cult known as "Aum Shinrikyo." Twelve people died in the attack, and over 5,000 were injured. The nerve gas used had been developed by Nazi scientists, and its effects were devastating when released in that crowded Tokyo subway during the morning peak hour of traffic.

After the attack, the Japanese police raided the headquarters of the cult, and they found enough of this poison gas to kill 10 million people—virtually the whole population of Tokyo. The cult also had massive assets worldwide, valued at over a billion dollars. In addition, they had stockpiled vast quantities of other germ warfare agents, and they had tried to secure atomic weapons as well as the dreadful Ebola virus (from Zaire).

Michael Drosnin tells us that the details of this event are encoded in the Bible. The words "Aum Shinrikyo" were found encoded with the words "subway," "gas"(twice), and "plague." Other words supposedly encoded were "Tokyo," "Japan," "cyanide," "airplane squadron," and "flying weapons." However, these translations are highly suspect.

There is a problem with taking a language such as English and foisting it on to a quite different language (Hebrew).

Thus, when we come to Drosnin's discussion about Kobe and Japan (pp. 107, 145, 167), we have to accept that "Japan" can be written as "yod-pe-nun" (twice intercrossing at p. 107).

Then there's the word "Kobe." On page 145 of his book Drosnin tells us that (transliterated) K- plus the vowel marker, then V or B-H- [i.e., Kobe], plus Y-P-N- [Japan] should be translated as Kobe, Japan—written backwards in the Hebrew script. However, the letters present in the Hebrew text could be used to make other names. That is, Kobe isn't the only possible translation.

The Oklahoma Bombing

Another example of Drosnin's selective approach to transliteration is found in his words about the Oklahoma bombing. Drosnin gives us specific details about that horrible act of terror, starting with the murderer—"his name is Timothy." Then in a separate series of "skip sequences" on the same extracted page, "McVeigh" is added, with a "skip sequence" of five letters. Those letters are, in English equivalents to the Hebrew, M-K-Wau ("wau" can be V), wau again (which can also be a "vowel marker") -yod which again can (in a sense) be part of a vowel marker, and finally another yod.

In view of the dramatic claim based on the actual name of the terrorist being foretold in the Bible, one would expect the name to be much more clearly delineated than is the case before us. In actuality, Drosnin's transliteration is stretched to accommodate the phonetically difficult word "McVeigh." MKVau could be translated as several different names—Makvau, Mckvau, and so on. *McVeigh* is only an interpretation based on the assumption of an accurate Bible code that predicts future events. In any case, it is doubtful if any Hebrew scholar would offer (in English equivalents) m-k-w-y-y- as the best way to transliterate the name "McVeigh."

On page 177 of Drosnin's book, in reference to the Oklahoma bombing, we find an extra consonant on the end of

"Oklahoma" as though the word were spelled ending with an "h." This is understandable linguistically, but it is not convincing.

Other Examples

There are other examples like this, such as "L.A. Calif" on page 41 of Drosnin's book, supposedly referring to Los Angeles, California. Such an interpretation suggests that the Bible code was written especially for an era in which the short abbreviation L.A. came into popular usage.

Even Drosnin's sensational reference to the Arab leader Arafat in conjunction with "the end of days" (page 171) can be challenged, as there is no vowel marker after the letter that is the equivalent of our English "f." Such a vowel marker could be omitted, but at other places where it fits Drosnin's approach, he uses them freely. It is possible to argue that this is legitimate, but it again points to the indefiniteness of such adaptations from Hebrew to English.

Significant Mistranslations

Ronald Hendel in his article, "The Secret Code," printed in *Bible Review* (August 1997) mentions several significant mistranslations that Drosnin makes:

- "After the death of Abraham" (Genesis 25:11) is rendered "After the death (of) Prime Minister" (page 58).

- "Which she [Rebekah] had made" (Genesis 27:17) is rendered "fire, earthquake" (page 142).

- "[You] will be my people. I am [Yahweh your God]" (Leviticus 26:1-13) is rendered as "July to Amman" (page 157).

- "[The men] numbered by Moses" (Numbers 26:64) is rendered as "code will save" (page 180).

As Drs. Clifford and Barbara Wilson have pointed out in all these examples of textual and translation problems, we have good reason to approach Drosnin's interpretations with caution and even doubt. There are additional examples that could be cited, but the ones we've reviewed give us a good cross-section of the problems that are present in *The Bible Code*.

The Code and the Autographs

One potential problem for the Bible code is the need for a virtually autographic text—that is, the Bible text as originally written by Moses—or a flawless copy of the original text. A text that is not autographic would of necessity invalidate any supposedly divinely instituted code, based on a strict skip sequence. Drosnin himself agrees that this is the only way the code could work. He claims, "All Bibles in the original Hebrew language that now exist are the same letter for letter."[32]

This, however, is simply not the case. Any Hebrew textual scholar will confirm that Drosnin is wrong. As Ronald S. Hendel writes:

> Hebrew spelling practices were not uniformly fixed. In some biblical texts vowel letters . . . are used in a given word while in other texts they may be absent from the word. . . . These differences in spelling make no difference in the meaning of the word; they are just alternative spellings. As a result of these differences every known ancient Hebrew manuscript of the Bible, including every manuscript of the traditional Masoretic text, has a different number of letters. This is a fatal problem for a computer program that relies on the manipulation of exact numerical sequences of letters. Which manuscript or edition should be used for such a program?[33]

Drosnin himself mentioned this problem. On the "Oprah Winfrey Show" he was explaining why the code can be found only in the Hebrew Bible and not in any other translation. He stated, "Once you take a code and change all the words, as you do when you make any translation, *the code disappears*"[34] (emphasis added).

If no Hebrew manuscripts are the same letter for letter, then, critics allege, "the code disappears" *unless* the version Rips used is autographic. But no one can prove that without the availability of the autographs themselves. Unfortunately, no one has them or knows where to find them. Most likely, they are irretrievably lost.

One critical article points out the problems involved in attempting to verify the Bible code while using a less than 100 percent perfect text: 1) if there were only 100 copying and format differences between the autographic Pentateuch and the modern versions: and these 2) resulted in the dropping of a letter here, adding of a letter there, changing one word to another word of another line, dropping a word, adding a word, etc.; and that 3) these differences were more or less evenly distributed throughout the Pentateuch; and 4) assuming God had encoded messages in the original text; then 5) a run of the ELS computer program that started at a point in the Pentateuch would stumble after it had only gone about 1 percent further in the text. "All analysis after that point would be meaningless because the ELS would initially be out of synchronization by one or more characters."[35]

Serious code researchers respond by saying that a perfect text is not needed to verify the legitimacy of the Bible code. They argue that the code deteriorates proportionately to the number of missing or altered letters but that the system has a degree of tolerance built into it. In other words, it can accommodate a very limited number of errors before becoming entirely garbled.[36] Satinover argues as follows: "If the text does get changed, but not too much, the codes will *not* disappear. The more errors that creep in, the more the Bible code loses its robustness, not being entirely effaced until a critical number of mistakes has occurred."[37]

Witztum, Rips, and Rosenberg (and later Gans) all agree that the critical point is the loss of one letter per every 1,000 letters, or a total of 78 letters for the 78,000-letter text of Genesis. Witztum, Rips, and Rosenberg showed this in a control study with deliberately deleted letters: "as the change consisted exclusively of [77] deletions, each deletion 'hit the frame' of the subsequent text, progressively causing the count for every successive code to be further off. As in the aging of DNA, a deletion causes worse damage to a code [on average] than does substitution."[38] In his own experiment, Gans later agreed: "Several experiments which I performed indicate that the error rate that is necessary to obliterate the statistical significance of the codes is about one deleted letter for every 1000 letters (78 letters)."[39]

It is arguably the case that the extremely small number of alterations in the different versions of the Torah does not erase the Bible code—assuming it is there. But it will damage it to some degree. Between the traditional Jewish (Koren) text used by Jews worldwide and the *Biblia Hebraica Stuttgartensis* (BHS), the standard critical text used by biblical scholars, there are 130-plus differences in the entire Pentateuch. In Genesis, the Koren edition differs from the BHS in only 23 places—one word break difference, four deletions, five substitutions, and 13 additions.[40] Of course, even in the Pentateuch as a whole, not all 130 differences deal with deletions. Thus, assuming the superiority of the Koren text, Satinover argues that the code should also be present in the BHS text, although not quite so robustly. He argues, "That is precisely what later results have shown."[41] But is must not be forgotten that unless the Koren edition used is autographic, at least some degree of corruption will occur in the code—of necessity. And, this raises problems for accurately interpreting the code. As Satinover remarks, "change 'color' to 'colour' and *everything* that follows is shifted one letter out of sequence."[42] If so, it is hard to see how any reliable code at all can continue to remain. Among the three Torahs used worldwide by the Jews "there are only 9 variations *total* in the *entire* 300,000-letter text—in other words, a very low .002%."[43] While if true, this suggests the Jewish Torah may be more accurate than the critical *Biblia Hebraica* text, it still leaves serious problems for a code dependent on the autographs.

Again, we will have to see how critics respond to these claims that some alteration "tolerance" is built into the codes. As Satinover says of this, "The debate will not really become fully engaged until critical pieces are published, which will then open the door for further rebuttal by the original authors, replication by others, and new extensions of the method. This is all brewing at the moment."[44]

This raises an interesting point. As noted, the different versions of Hebrew Bibles have slight variations. For example, the Leningrad Codex, the basis for *Biblia Hebraica*, differs from the version Drosnin used by 41 letters in Deuteronomy.[45] Even with *different* versions available, are people still finding Bible code messages? More research needs to be done, but if codes were still found, we would hardly be surprised because the Hebrew language, when so easily subjected to manipulation by computer, easily lends itself to finding messages.

Other Textual Issues

When we consider the textual history of ancient Hebrew we encounter more problems. Hebrew spelling, like that of Shakespearean English or other older languages, was never completely uniform. Minor variations in spelling existed, which would lead to different numbers of letters in a given word. In addition, as Hendel points out, biblical texts written before the sixth century B.C. also had fewer letters than our earliest Hebrew biblical manuscripts:

> A Hebrew manuscript from the time of Moses would
> have used no vowel letters at all because vowel letters
> were not introduced into Hebrew until the ninth to
> eighth centuries B.C. So one can't count the letters in
> any of our Hebrew manuscripts and presume that
> the letter count is the original. The original was
> shorter.[46]

Unfortunately, the problem becomes more complex. In
Drosnin's appendix, "Notes on Illustrations," he says that it is
sometimes possible to use slightly different word breaks
between the existing Hebrew letters and come up with an
entirely new sentence. He also says that the Bible code sometimes uses a condensed form of Hebrew:

> Sometimes the original text of the Bible, with only
> slightly different word breaks between the existing
> letters, reveals precise information about events in
> the modern world. . . . In some cases the Bible code
> uses a condensed form of Hebrew, as one would
> expect in a code. And the Bible code, like the Bible
> itself, sometimes drops letters that are generally used
> in modern Hebrew, primarily the vuv and the yud. [47]

Drosnin shows what happens when one changes the
breaks between the letters in Numbers 3:24. The original text
of this verse reads, "the chief of the house of the father of the
Gershonites." However, by placing the word breaks in different places, the sentence can be made to read, "President,
but he was kicked out."

This raises an important question: How can we know
when it's appropriate to change the word breaks in the original Hebrew text? Isn't there always the danger that we could
create contrived or incorrect readings by imposing new word
breaks at whim?

Also, is it surprising that in a text the size of the Old Testament the word "Watergate" could be found in code? No. Is

it surprising that a manipulation of the text could reveal "President" and "kicked out"? Again, no.

Too Much Uncertainty?

In *The Bible Code*, Drosnin persuasively presents his interpretations of what the Bible code is telling us. But upon closer scrutiny, we see that criticisms can be leveled against these interpretations. What's more, these problems affect not just isolated portions of the Bible code, but they do significant damage to the whole case for the code as presented by Drosnin.

While words and names may appear to be coded in the Hebrew text as researched by Rips, Witztum, and Drosnin, we must be extremely careful about attempts to deduce messages or prophecies from those words. Doing so takes us into the realms of translation and interpretation, and as we've seen in this chapter, there are still too many unanswered questions for us to determine exactly what, if anything, is being communicated by the code. After all, in the previous chapter we learned that hidden words can be found in texts other than the Bible, and we can be certain that those words were not intentionally encoded into those texts. Also, it's difficult to place confidence in a code that contradicts the plain reading of the Bible. Then there are the textual issues, involving matters such as the variations in the numbers of letters present in different Hebrew manuscripts, and the attempts to interpret a set of Hebrew letters one way when they could actually be interpreted several different ways.

More and more, we are seeing that there are definite uncertainties surrounding the whole phenomenon of the Bible Code. Isn't it interesting, by contrast, that we can be far more certain about what the plain text of the Bible says?

6

Problems Within
the Bible Code

Every scientist, every mathematician and physicist who understands the code, agrees that not even the fastest super-computers we have today—not all the Crays in the war room of the Pentagon, or all the mainframes at IBM, not all of the computers in the world now working together—could have encoded the Bible in the way it was done 3000 years ago. "I can't even imagine how it would be done, or how anyone could have done it," says Rips. "It's a mind beyond our imagination."[1]

That's a remarkable statement to make about the Bible code, especially when we consider that the research done so far has been limited in scope. Keep in mind that Witztum and Rips used only the book of Genesis in their original experiment. They believe that the entire Torah is encoded, but they have not yet published results on the remaining four books. Drosnin believes the entire Old Testament is coded and suggests that Rips and others, in part, may also believe this:

"I would be surprised if the same code we proved existed in Genesis did not exist in the rest of the Torah," states Rips. And he agrees that other parts of the Old Testament, like Daniel and Isaiah, might also be encoded. . . . The Bible code itself appears to confirm that the entire Old Testament is encoded. "He encoded the Torah, and more," states the code, evidence that not only the first five books, but at least some of the later writings also have hidden information.[2]

"Infinite" Data Encoded?

If the entire Old Testament is encoded, that means it's possible for an incredible amount of information to be hidden within the text. If there are literally billions upon billions of letter combinations in the Hebrew Bible, endless numbers of additional forms of "matrixes," and if the incredibly complex system of Bible codes developed by Rips et al is only the tip of the iceberg, then conceivably there could be an "infinite" number of letter combinations, "matrixes," and so on, that could, proponents argue, contain all the information in recorded and unrecorded history—past, present, and future.

Earlier we cited the Gaon of Vilna, who said that the "details of details of everything that happened" to every individual who ever lived, from the day of his birth until the day of his death, is recorded in the Torah:

> The rule is that all that was, is, and will be unto the end of time, is included in the Torah, from the first word to the last word. And not merely in a general sense, but as to the details of every species and each one individually, and details of details of everything that happened to him from the day of his birth until his end.[3]

Note that the Gaon specifically declares that "all that . . . *will be*" is encoded in the Torah. He specifically declares that the Torah, in code, predicts the future in detail. He claims the

Torah predicts not just broad outlines or a relatively "small" number of specific events as in the plain text of the Bible, but *all* the particular details of every person's future.

If further research proves beyond doubt that some kind of hidden code exists in the Bible and the code really does predict the future in detail, think of the implications. The Bible could become the greatest divination tool of all time. One can imagine how millions of people might search the code for information about their future so that they could avert disaster and control their destinies. Some people might even come up with bizarre applications, such as using codes to find out private information about others, or, in occult situations, find out more about their alleged past lives. Now, Drosnin doesn't advocate that's what could happen. Drosnin says that the encoded information about the future may deal more with possible outcomes rather than actual.

Exactly how much information can we expect to find hidden in the Bible? Drosnin says, "According to Rips there is an infinite amount of information encoded in the Bible. Each time a new name or word or phrase is discovered in the code, *a new crossword puzzle [matrix] is found.*"[4]

Elsewhere, Drosnin tells us:

> I asked Rips if there was any limit to the information that was in the code, how much of our history was hidden in the Bible. "Everything," said the mathematician [quoting Gaon of Vilna]. "All that was, is, and will be unto the end of time is included in the Torah."

> How could that be possible, the original text of the Old Testament was only 304,805 letters long?

> "Theoretically, there is no limit to the amount of information that could be encoded," said Rips . . . [after citing mathematical formulas to illustrate]. "In the end," says Rips, "the amount of information is

incalculable, and probably infinite. And that is only
the first, crudest level of the Bible code."[5]

In fact, Rips proceeds to argue, "It is almost certainly more
levels deep, but we do not yet have a powerful enough mathematical model to reach it. . . . It is probably less like a crossword puzzle, and more like a hologram. We are only looking
at two-dimensional arrays, and we probably should be
looking at three dimensions, but we don't know how to."[6]

Satinover also implies that the Bible codes contain infinite
knowledge[7] and are multilevel—"the codes were but one face
of a dazzling multifaceted jewel with depths beyond understanding."[8] Billions of skip codes, leading to billions of messages, and even different levels and dimensions. All this
boggles the mind.

Where Will It Lead?

If there truly is an infinite amount of information present
in the code, it would be possible for people to derive an infinite number of messages from it. People could even convince
themselves that these are "messages from God" intended just
for them. People could find virtually any message they
wished, justifying all sorts of self-serving behavior. Naturally,
people will pick out the messages they like, just as they frequently do with the Bible's surface content. This raises some
possible dangers: What if unbalanced people or people with
personal agendas see messages to harm or kill others or
commit suicide or swindle a partner or divorce a spouse or
commit adultery? What about defrauding the government,
planting a bomb, or killing a troublesome neighbor's cat or
dog? The kinds of messages people could find are seemingly
endless. Even Rips is concerned: "The worst thing that could
happen is that some people might interpret what they find in
the Bible code as commandments, as telling them what to
do. . . ."[9]

What if the Bible code phenomenon really becomes a national craze? We can imagine home computer programs being developed to get around the problem of people who don't know Hebrew. We can imagine simplified "code kits" that allow people to sift through the Bible to find "coded" information about almost anything. If the interest is there, the money-makers will market it.

Inherent Complexities

Another difficulty, not only for the layman but even the expert, is the code's extreme complexities and subtleties. Indeed, if only a few experts worldwide can understand these, it becomes a phenomenon that everyone else has to take on faith—that is, faith that the experts' claims are true. This is one of the troubling aspects of the codes—that you have to be an "expert's expert" so to speak to "verify" them. In fact, Doron Witztum himself went so far as to claim that "he alone could properly conduct code searches."[10] While Satinover argues that a certain feature of the decoding process explains Witztum's claim to exclusivity, such a claim is troubling nonetheless. Consider the following statements by Satinover as an illustration of code problems relative to their complexities:

> There are indeed certain subtleties to the codes that would make it quite difficult for just anyone to succeed in replicating them *even if* they have the technical aspect down pat. This elusiveness is what will unfold in this book; it should serve as both caution to hasty skeptics and hasty enthusiasts. The codes are powerful, but they are also subtle, and not so easy to verify[11] (emphasis added).

In fact, they are "very difficult" to verify and as we observed elsewhere, seem to have an elusive "quantum mechanical" aspect built right in:

The fact is that the methodology is *so subtle* that a valid statistical assessment—of the kind that would meet the standards of the toughest and most sophisticated critics—may be *somewhat beyond* even the heightened scientific skill of both Witztum (in theoretical physics) and Rips (in pure mathematics).

It barely fell well within the capabilities of the *most specialized and advanced statistical theory.* (As we will discuss later, many of the *highest-powered critics* acknowledge that their own skills may be insufficient to perform the necessary analysis)[12] (emphasis added).

If it takes extremely highly qualified people to properly evaluate the pros and cons of the research, then it is obvious that this debate is going to continue for some time. The mercurial nature of such code subtleties opens a potential Pandora's box for future research. If the Bible code is *full* of such subtleties, one can only guess at the outcome.

The difficulty with making the code widely accessible is that most people can't possibly know how to use the "real" code because of its inherent complexities. All they would get in terms of messages would be false or contrived. Mechanic, Witztum, and Gans also emphasize that distinguishing true codes from chance configurations requires an expertise beyond the average person's ability:

The *only* way one can objectively demonstrate that a word pattern was deliberately encoded in a document, rather than it being an accidental appearance, is through an objective, scientific and statistical evaluation. Because this evaluation depends on extremely complex mathematical and statistical computations *the great majority of people are incapable of making this evaluation.*[13]

How many people are going to submit their code findings to experts for a weeks- or months-long evaluation process to make certain they have found legitimate encoding? Even Drosnin came across false codes or contrived messages, yet he spent five years studying the phenomenon, took the time to learn Hebrew, and had personal access to the scholarly originators of the code system. How can the average person possibly fare any better?

But there is a more serious problem that affects any use of the code, either by experts or laymen.

Issues Related to Proper Interpretation

The greatest problem with the Bible code as it relates to the future is found at the level of interpretation. Because this issue is so crucial we will spend some time here. Let's begin with Drosnin's book and then proceed to what others have stated.

As we read Drosnin's book, it becomes difficult to know exactly what to believe concerning the code's ability to unravel our collective (or personal) futures. Drosnin is convinced the Bible was encoded by highly advanced alien intelligences, entities supposedly concerned with the collective welfare of humanity (a common UFO "contactee" theme). The aliens intended the code to be broken at the right time, to warn us about things like nuclear war and Armageddon. So it would seem logical that using the code to ascertain our future is central to the code designer's purposes. Here is where we open a Pandora's box.

To Delay or Not to Delay

First, we have the concept of "delay" written into the code—presumably because people have the freedom to act in ways that may change the outcomes of events prophesied in the code.

Although there are a few examples of this phenomenon in the surface text of the Bible, as with the prophet Jonah's prophecy to Nineveh, the vast majority of biblical prophecies deal with concrete predictions of events that have a predetermined outcome. To think of Bible prophecy as generally indeterminate is to destroy the meaning of prophecy. For Christians, whether Christ might or might not have been crucified or might or might not return would have significant ramifications on Christian beliefs and teachings.

Unfortunately, this concept of delay is found frequently in Drosnin's book. The insuperable difficulty is devising a way to objectively interpret the code so that the warnings may be heeded in the way that they should be.

Consider some illustrations:[14]

- "Delay" is written into the Bible and the code

- "Delay" is written in with "year of the plague"

- "Delay" is written in with "World War"

- "When Moses tells the ancient Israelites what will happen in the 'End of Days,' the hidden text appears to say 'delayed'"

- "The words that are encoded with both 'atomic holocaust' and 'World War'—the hidden text states 'friend delayed'"

- "'Delay' is written into all the original prophecies of the 'End of Days'"

To warn of international disasters and to simultaneously speak of "delay" seems an obvious attempt to influence people's behavior. But how should we interpret such warnings and delays? Are we to believe that God has (for predetermined events) already delayed the fulfillment of the prediction? Or is it up to us to do so? Or should we trust that alien intelligences ("friend delayed"?) will step in behind the scenes and delay the fulfillment of the prophecies?

Enigmas and Riddles

If *everything* can be delayed, and in some cases we cannot even determine if the prophecy is speaking of a delay *or not,* what's the point of a prophecy to begin with? If everything is only a probability, actual *prediction* of the future is impossible. And then one begins to wonder if the inventor of the code is really omniscient. Or is he just mischievous? Unless it is God speaking clearly, all bets are off. It's one thing for God to tell us that a prophecy of judgment can be delayed if people repent of their evil, as was the case for the city of Nineveh. It's another thing entirely for people to assume the same from an alleged Bible code that no one knows quite how to interpret. It's one thing to avert a disaster accurately predicted in advance, as with satellite hurricane warnings. It's something else entirely for people or institutions or nations to go to lengths to avert a guess about the future. That's when the code becomes dangerous.

Concerning the great earthquake that will allegedly hit Los Angeles in the year 2010, even though the Bible code predicts it, Drosnin says it's still "only a probability."[15] Didn't we already know that?

Further, if we *can* control some of the possible outcomes or avert them, why would Bible code predictions of natural disasters over which humans have *no* control, such as earthquakes, be considered only probabilities? Does the author of the Bible code know the future or not?

Concerning the Apocalypse in the book of Revelation, and its associated phenomena (great earthquakes, and so on), we read, "It is *not clear* if the code is stating a series of disasters, or a series of delays." So what are mortals to conclude? Which will it be so that we may know what to do?

A Changing Code

Even Drosnin himself is unable to be fully certain of the warnings that appear in the Bible code. In response to events he was observing, he said, "The Bible code seemed to be updating itself almost as if the encoder were also following the constant turn of events in the Middle East. One location was encoded over the other, one crisis over another, one year over another, so that finally there was *no way* to *be certain* if the real danger was in 1996, 1997 or the year 2000 *or beyond*. But the overall danger was very clearly stated. . . . "[16]

Goodness, what difference does it make at all if an "overall danger was very clearly stated" only *at some unknown time* in the future? What good does that do anyone?

If we assume the danger is *for* the year 2000, may not our actions actually precipitate the crisis since we did not wait for the "some point beyond," the time at which proper action was really needed? What if we assume the danger is *beyond* 2000, only to find out that the real danger really does take place *at* the year 2000?

Can anyone imagine *God* "clearly" telling us, "Be warned! There may *or may not* be a nuclear holocaust that will destroy the world. It may *or may not* happen at some point in the future." Who would know what to do?

But things get even more interesting when we read that in one Bible code an interwoven hidden text declares, "Five futures, five roads."[17] There is no ambiguity or enigma here. It is hardly surprising that Drosnin finally concludes, "It may be impossible to know both what and when."[18] If so, then what's the point of a code?

Further, consider what Rips believes about the code. He argues that the entire code had to be written at once, in a single flash, but that "we experience it like we experience a hologram—it looks different when we look at it from a new angle. . . ."[19] If what Rips says is true, then the code is meaningless. If the code is constantly changing, if it looks different from different angles, if it has a variety of levels and we are only at the first level, and if there is an obvious subjective element in interpreting the code messages, then again, of what relevance is the code? It can mean anything to anyone, or give contradictory messages both at "surface" and "higher" levels.

A Useless Intelligence Report?

Now, consider the following statement from Drosnin and Rips, and ask yourself once more: Of what value is the code?

> [The Bible code] is the history of the human race recorded more than 3000 years ahead of time. It does not tell the story sequentially, but all at once. Modern events overlap ancient events, the future is encoded in verses that tell of the biblical past. One verse might contain within it the stories of then and now and a hundred years from now. "The problem is how we decipher it all," said Rips. "It is clearly non-random, but it is as if we had an intelligence report in which we can read only one of every twenty words."[20]

How interesting: Here we have a code—supposedly an intelligence report—revealing crucial information concerning our lives and futures, and we can only read one word in 20, if that. If the reader wishes, he may take a black felt-tip pen, blot out 19 of every 20 words on any page in this book, and then try and read it. How could anyone possibly know the interpretation or even the relevance of what remained? How can Rips possibly conclude that a code is meaningful if it is like an intelligence report in which we can only read five percent of the words?

Still, Rips is convinced that the code is the product of a higher intelligence (God). But then he goes on to state, "It may want us to understand, but it may not want us to understand."[21] The code is so preferential that it "may not reveal the future to us unless we are worthy."[22]

This opens up a new can of worms. Who is worthy? Is one person who is presumably more worthy than another going to find out more information or going to interpret the code more accurately than another less worthy? Are the true "interpreters of the future" going to be only those who are "worthy"? By whose standards?

Drosnin's conclusion to his book underscores the overall dilemma for believers in the code: "Is the Bible code merely giving a scientific gloss to millennium fever, or is it warning us, perhaps just in time, of a very real danger? There is no way to know." If there is "no way to know," wouldn't it be dangerous to count on the code as being valid? Drosnin goes on to say, "The code may be neither 'right' nor 'wrong.'"[23] How does a person trust a code he or she cannot trust to speak clearly?

It's looking more and more like God might not be the author of the code. Rips had said that even though the Bible was encoded by one mind, it may "encode two different points of view." In fact, it may encode a thousand different points of view! No one can say it doesn't. But clearly, according to the plain text of the Bible, God is not a God who says both "yes" and "no" at the same time, nor is He a God of confusion.

> "God is not a God of confusion" (1 Corinthians 14:33 NASB).

> When I planned this, did I do it lightly? Or do I make my plans in a worldly manner so that in the same breath I say, "Yes, yes" and "No, no"? But as surely as God is faithful, our message to you is not "Yes" and "No" (2 Corinthians 1:17-19).

Multiple Meanings

Consider Drosnin's examples of codes that have multiple messages. In one code referring to the world war that never happened in 1995–1996 we find the words "plague," "peace," and "save." When it comes to Armageddon, who is going to interpret *that* properly?[24]

When Drosnin cites Exodus 32:16, referring to God's writing the Ten Commandments on tablets of stone, he finds a hidden message, "It was made by computer."[25] Why does Drosnin interpret the "it" as referring to the tablets, rather than to the code itself? After all, Exodus 32:16 is a reference to the recording of divine revelation. And if the code is a *new* revelation from God, "it" could just as easily refer to the code being made by a computer. Or, "it" could mean a dozen different things. Who knows what "it" is? Only the author of the code, whoever that may be.

Another problem can be seen in the range of meaning found behind words that are the same. Drosnin has a Hebrew letter matrix predicting a great Los Angeles earthquake for the year 2010. The code reads "great earthquake." But in the same code we find an alleged prediction of the January 1994 Los Angeles/Northridge earthquake that killed 61 people. The term "great earthquake" is also applied to this earthquake, which was relatively minor compared to the predicted cataclysm of the great earthquake that scientists agree will one day strike Southern California. Even Drosnin himself admits the 1994 quake was barely a tremor compared to what is expected to come. If the code uses the term "great" to describe both large and small in relative proportions, how can we properly interpret the message? Will the "big one" that experts expect to hit California in the next 40 years merely be a relatively *minor* earthquake killing only a few tens of people? Regardless, "it is only a probability,"[26] says Drosnin.

Does the Bible Code Really Know?

In Drosnin's efforts to sort through the alleged predictions in the Bible code, he states, "It also seemed a clear statement [from the code] that there were many possible futures, that the Bible code revealed each of them."[27] So who interprets which future is which? Perhaps Drosnin's very next statement is the question he should have asked himself more soberly: "Why didn't the Bible code just tell us the final outcome—the one real future?"[28]

Indeed, why not? The whole matter of multiple possibilities makes it seem as if the code is playing games with us. Why would God do that? And, if the Bible code *is* divine revelation, do we then assume that all the predictions in the Old and New Testaments are equally uncertain? Maybe God doesn't know the future after all? Or, maybe the Bible really is a product of alien intelligence, as Von Daniken and others claim—and we haven't been able to determine how to make complete sense of it? Maybe the Bible code is a prelude to alien contact, as some argue?

Handling the Hebrew Text

The above discussions show why the most consistent objection to the Bible code is one of interpretation. One critic writes,

> Almost every word in Hebrew can be interpreted as either a noun or a verb, depending on the surrounding context or as indicated by any prefixes, or modifiers used. This means that innumerable passages can be read in different ways. While the ancient Hebrew written language is very efficient, it leads to massive amounts of misunderstanding. . . . Since many words are only three letters long, it makes it relatively easy to find hidden words using a skip code. There would be far more word matches in an ancient Hebrew text than in an English text with the same number of pages. Also, since words were usually written without vowels, and nouns and verbs were often identical, Drosnin's interpretation of any nearby letter combinations could take many forms.[29]

In addition, an article in *Bible Review* pointed out that Rips and Witztum's definition of "near" seems arbitrary. Concerning the dates they found for the deaths of the famous rabbis, "in many cases, the death dates found by this method are nearer to a different rabbi from the one to whom the death date applies."[30]

Bruce Wilner is an electrical engineer, mathematician, linguist, and computer scientist with a significant background in pattern recognition. He entered a paper on the internet, entitled "An Impartial Opinion of the 'Torah codes.'" In that paper he pointed out the following:

> A friend of mine who is quite fluent in Hebrew was unable to interpret many of the passages in the way that the book indicates without, shall we say, a generous dose of poetic license. It is also disturbing that some of the passages must be read forward, others backward, while one[31] ["it was made by computer"] evidently reads boustrophedonically! Some of the passages that Drosnin refers to in his appendix did not match the versions in any of my Bible translations.
>
> Hebrew is so prone to wordplay it is utterly ridiculous. Because of the triconsonantal rule, many words are extremely short, so a given snippet of text with spaces between the words removed could be interpreted in innumerable ways.[32]

Consider Drosnin's mistranslation of the "assassin who will assassinate" code. Even this mistranslation can be read in different ways. Perhaps it meant that, as Rabin's political critics alleged, Rabin was an assassin who killed Israelis by pursuing peace. "Relationships are indeed in the eye of the beholder."[33] Dr. Satinover pointed out on the Oprah Winfrey show that the phrase "assassin will assassinate" also has "seven other phrases open to interpretation that equally well run through that name."[34]

Perhaps this is why the commentary section for *Business Week* (June 16, 1997), titled "He Who Mines Data May Strike Fools Gold," says that Drosnin's code methodology is so bad it is still valuable as an example about how *not* to read data.[35]

Rabbi Daniel Mechanic comments on Drosnin's prediction of Watergate, and says that even if you accept that word,

"There is no Hebrew word here that means 'who is he?'" and, "To have half the code in English and the other half in Hebrew is insane. There is no mathematical or statistical validity here."[36]

Making Sense of the Findings

Another question is this: How can Rips, Witztum, and others criticize Drosnin for using the same or a similar methodology to their own? Doron Witztum is correct when he argues, "All we have [in Drosnin's predictive Bible codes] is a few isolated encoded words of a hidden text. Maybe we are missing some very critical words? It's literally impossible to learn a coherent story out of the juxtaposition of a few words that may somehow be related."[37]

Gans, who confirmed the original *Statistical Science* research, agrees: "Looking for four or five key words makes no sense. You cannot develop a meaningful statistic on it."[38] Here, the principals seem to criticize what even Rips and other serious researchers have done with the Bible code. Drosnin, in his book, stated that Rips at several points agreed with him in his now allegedly unjustified use and interpretation of the code.

The *Jerusalem Post* notes that (apparently during their interview) Rips entered the title of a book about the Gaon of Vilna into the computer. In just a few seconds Gaon's name appeared at 12,315 letters from the beginning, while "Vilna" appeared very close to it. In one or two other references, "Vilna" overlapped the book's title.[39] Isn't this the same method Drosnin used?

The apparent difficulty is that Rips, Witztum, and Drosnin all seem to be using, at least to a significant degree, the same *kind* of methodology. An article in *Newsweek* magazine first cited Rips's denial of Drosnin's book (saying that the book had no value). The author says next, "Yet the Bible code finds its startling matches much the same way as Rips found the encrypted names of the Jewish sages."[40] How then can Drosnin be condemned for using a method similar to what Rips used?

In other words, in exactly what ways is Drosnin's methodology the same or different from that of Rips, et al? This needs much greater clarification.

As we noted earlier, one of the difficulties for codes research is the extreme subtleties involved. We cited Witztum's claim that "he alone could properly conduct code searches" because "no one else fully understood his variation of the decoding method."[41] Thus Robert Haralick is another independent code researcher who "has presented various findings using somewhat different techniques than those" of the principals. Indeed, "there is substantial disagreement between him and other codes researchers about his methodology. But it would be fair to say that he is a qualified disputant, and there will necessarily emerge a wide range of opinion and approaches as the phenomenon becomes more widely known."[42] Drosnin, of course, has his approach to the codes as well. And we received the following e-mail communication from serious internet code researchers: "We have several researchers on the code who are experimenting with different methods of code research—progressive skips, unequal ELSs, etc., looking for what we believe should be unambiguous sentences encoded rather than just ambiguous word pairs." This seemingly elastic and subjective element is very troubling—especially when "the mathematical assessments about the code are still being debated."[43]

Dr. Satinover points out only some of the complexities involved in assessing the code: one, how the sets of data were selected and structured and the relative strengths and weaknesses or overall merit of the approach; two, assessing the legitimacy of alternative selection methods and formats; three, problems involved with in the "compactness measure itself" and how the results it gives compares with alternatives; four, what direction future research should take and how it should be structured; and so on. "All this is likely to take a few years of increasingly sophisticated back-and-forth."[44]

Indeed. Serious research is just now beginning and the phenomena are so subtle and complex that the most we can ask at this point is whether sufficient quality evidence exists to warrant further investigation. Satinover himself agrees:

> If the letters of the Torah really do form a blueprint "map" it is not the one-to-one mapping of an architect's drawing of a house; it is more like the map of a lifetime contained in the thoughts of the mind. In regard to the Bible code, this means that it may be *exceedingly difficult* to show that any individual ELS combination is unlikely. . . . Such broad trends would require long and arduous investigation whether to confirm or refute convincingly. The evidence so far suggests if the Bible code exists, it is precisely of that sort. Serious investigation is therefore really only in its infancy. In fact, from the point of view of science, the "argument" amounts to, "Is there sufficient evidence of adequate quality to date, to warrant further investigation?"[45] (emphasis added).

Who Has the Key?

A final serious and, to our way of thinking, fatal problem is that we really don't have the "key" to the code. If there really were a code from God, would He not give us the key to interpreting the code properly, rather than leave us on our own? If He really does want us to do the right thing and prevent these kinds of disasters, then certainly He would have supplied the key to the very code He presumably is now revealing. But He did not. What does this say? Until we have the key, we have no idea of who or what we are dealing with—if anything.

Anyone who has opened a box holding a gigantic jigsaw puzzle and poured all the little pieces onto a table knows the initial sense of dread that comes when contemplating all the work that remains in order to piece together the entire puzzle. Putting together 100 pieces of a puzzle that has a million pieces will not give a person any idea of the entire picture. Worse, what if the manufacturer of the puzzle accidentally puts in pieces from 50 different puzzles? Or puts the wrong picture on the lid of the box? Even Rips has used the analogy of a jigsaw puzzle. In the words of Drosnin, "There is still a great deal no one knows about the Bible code. Rips, who *knows more than anyone,* says it is like a giant jigsaw puzzle with thousands of pieces, and we only have a few hundred."[46]

Perhaps the code actually has a billion pieces. Perhaps the real meaning of the Bible code will be found in the last 1,000 pieces? Perhaps the real "meaning" will be different from what anyone now thinks?

In the *Jerusalem Post,* Rips was quoted as saying this:

> The truth is that we're nowhere near solving the secret of what the key to the code is. It is far more complex, even [with] using the most powerful computers we possess today to solve its mystery. *We do not have the key.* The question remains: Between *knowing nothing* and knowing everything (if we ever get the key), is there an intermediate position? Is there anything we can say with the limited knowledge that we have now?

Rips next declares, "All we can say is that there is a code and it applies only to the Bible," because "we did not find it duplicated in any other Hebrew texts. . . ."[47]

Dr. Satinover also realizes the complexity involved concerning a "key" when he discusses ancient Kabbalistic tradition, different levels of encryption, and the need for objective rules for assessing the phenomena:

> Ancient [Kabbalistic] tradition holds that there are
> "seventy gates" of wisdom, seventy different methods
> of interpreting the text of the Torah. Of these skipping
> letters is one (according to the Zohar the fiftieth) but
> if the Vilna Gaon's previous claim that *all* the details
> of history are contained in the Torah—a text of only
> 300,000-plus letters—is correct, then the Bible code
> must use many different encryption schemes to
> accommodate them i.e. not only *equidistant steps;* not
> only minimal spacing, etc. But if there are many dif-
> ferent coding rules, there *must also be rules* to define
> which class of information is encrypted according to
> which rule[48] (latter emphasis added).

Dr. Satinover proceeds to discuss the problem for codes
research if things turn out otherwise and no "keys" or "rules"
are found:

> If the world at large is to take it seriously, the scientific
> world especially, the Bible code cannot remain some-
> thing that only one or two people are able to uncover.
> The "rules" that allow genuine statistically verifiable
> codes to be found must eventually be reduced to
> writing, however complex and nuanced they may
> prove to be. Without such "parameterization" the
> suspicion will continually arise that positive findings
> are merely the result of inadvertent "tuning and
> snooping" or worse; deliberate fraud.[49]

Indeed, what kind of conclusions can anyone possibly
make about a secret code that has a key to understanding
it . . . that no one has . . . that may not exist?

7

The Dangers of the Bible Code

I f it is eventually proven that the Bible code phenomenon exists, and that it cannot logically be explained apart from divine inspiration/omniscience, then a very powerful argument will be added to the Christian apologetic arsenal—probably the most powerful there is. Of course, the kinds of problems we have cited will need to be resolved before that can be the case.

Whatever the final outcome of the *Statistical Science* article and subsequent research now in progress, it is worth pointing out that this phenomenon suggesting divine authorship of the Torah has already proven unique. Never before has there been an attempt to use science in the defense of the metaphysical in general or the Bible in particular that has undergone such rigorous scientific examination as the Bible codes.

In part, this is the problem. Despite the expert testimonies given thus far, it will take years to either confirm or refute the existence of a Bible code. Yet millions of people are now learning of the alleged existence of a Bible code and are being convinced by the testimonials on its behalf. Many people are using their own computers in an attempt to discover future events or even their own personal futures. Even some Christians are citing the Bible code as the primary and most vital evidence that the Bible is the Word of God, and telling this to others.

However, if the Bible code is disproved some years from now, what are millions of people going to conclude about the credibility of Christians...or the Bible? To tie the credibility of the Bible to the Bible code could be very consequential.

Christians believe that Christian evidences already provide sufficient documentation that the Bible actually is God's revelation to mankind. Author John Weldon, a convert from skepticism and agnosticism, has offered some evidence for this in *Ready With an Answer* (1997), *Knowing the Truth About Salvation* (1997), and other works.

Christians must be careful not to accept something that is questionable, no matter how convincing it appears, when it impacts the Bible's credibility in the minds of Christians and an ever-watching world. The consequences could be significant. Unfortunately, many have accepted the Bible code as real and authoritative. In the following pages, we will offer reasons why Christians should not accept this phenomenon until proven—no matter how convincing it may seem.

The Danger of Incorrect Claims

Several published books and pamphlets written by Christians are saying that Bible codes offer "proof that the Bible is God's Word." Different evangelical Christian sites on the worldwide web claim these codes are "irrefutable scientific evidence that the Bible is God's Word" and that they also prove that "Jesus is the Messiah."

In the past, Christians have embarrassed themselves and even unintentionally discredited their faith by making claims that were later proven to be wrong. Allegedly, while on his deathbed, Charles Darwin repented of his theory of evolution and turned to Christ. This simply is not true, and besides, is irrelevant to the creation/evolution issue, which can be decided only on the basis of the scientific evidence *(see* Dr.

Weldon's *Darwin's Leap of Faith* [Eugene, OR: Harvest House, 1998]). Allegedly, the famous atheist Madalyn Murray O'Hair was involved in a plot of sorts to ban Christian programming from the airwaves. Literally millions of man-hours were and have been wasted in bombarding the FCC with petitions to prevent nonexistent legislation—the FCC still receives thousands of signed petitions yearly. Some people have claimed that the Proctor and Gamble company logo reveals that the company is satanic. This claim has cost Proctor and Gamble significant loss of revenue and led to other problems both for the company and those who continue to spread the rumors.

Whether a false claim is intriguing, exciting, or seemingly true is irrelevant. A false claim is a false claim—a lie. Lying is very clearly forbidden in the Bible (Colossians 3:9).

What Do the Codes Really Prove?

It is understandable how Christians could become stirred up over the issue of Bible codes. Evidence that confirms the faith is exciting. As we have seen, many claims have been made which appear to make the code legitimate. *Statistical Science* is a highly reputable journal; a six-year period review process is impressive. Independent scholarly confirmation is more impressive. Drosnin is an atheist skeptic who is yet convinced the code is real, and his book makes fascinating and convincing reading. But unless a person knows Hebrew and/or reads very critically, it is all too easy to be taken in and accept Drosnin's claims.

Again we must remember that outstanding claims require outstanding proofs. When we are dealing with something as important as the credibility and authority of Scripture, we must be very careful not to hold fast to claims that may not be true.

Telling the world that the codes are genuine and are actual proof of the divine inspiration of the Bible, or that they reveal absolute mathematical certainty that Jesus is the

Messiah is premature at best. Actually, it is a deception. First, while the initial research and response seems impressive, the code phenomenon is not yet proven—only time can bear it out. Second, the claim that Jesus' Messiahship is proven in the Old Testament through the codes is simply not true. While there is little doubt that the plain meaning of the Bible reveals that Jesus was and is the Jewish Messiah (the very existence of the Christian church—begun by Jews—can hardly be explained otherwise [see *The Case for Jesus the Messiah* by Dr. Ankerberg and John Weldon]), this has not yet been indicated in codes research. In fact, there are some serious problems with the claims being made by these people.

Examining the Claims

One of them, a popular evangelical author known in particular for his bestselling books on prophecy, wrote:

> ...the following material is the most thrilling revelation that I could share with my readers.... [God] has actually hidden the name *Yeshua,* which means Jesus, in numerous passages from Genesis to Malachi throughout the Old Testament. Especially within the great messianic prophetic passages God has hidden at equally spaced intervals in the Hebrew text the incredible message that "Yeshua is My Name." This is one of the most astonishing and tremendous Biblical discoveries in the last two thousand years.... Mathematical experts calculated [that] the probability of this astonishing combination, "Yeshua [Jesus] is My Name," would occur by random chance in this Messianic prophecy in Isaiah (53:10) is only one chance in 50 quadrillion, an inconceivable number!

The author goes on to claim that the serious Hebrew codes research generally is "one of the strongest proofs that the Bible was truly inspired by God."[1] These claims, to put it simply, are false.

Other authors have written entire books supplying seemingly legitimate and fascinating confirmation of the Christian messianic application of the Bible codes. The problem is that, based on the following analysis by code experts, none of it is true.

Exposing the Problems

The following material is excerpted from the public domain article "Jesus Codes: Uses and Abuses" by Rabbi Daniel Mechanic, Doron Witztum, and Harold Gans.[2] Remember, Harold Gans was a senior cryptologic mathematician for the government for almost 30 years. He was involved with the world's most advanced methods, experts, and facilities for the detection and decryption of encoded material, the author of 190 technical papers—a world-class expert in evaluating codes. Witztum is probably the preeminent codes researcher in the world. Therefore what these authors say deserves careful consideration.

The authors take issue with two texts in particular, and by extension many others of a similar genre which claim that codes research proves that Jesus is the Messiah. They claim that these books "reveal, unfortunately, a complete misunderstanding of the 'codes methodology,' how it works, and what can and cannot be asserted concerning them."

The authors point out that there are legitimate and illegitimate extrapolations that can be made from codes research. Obviously, only two types of meaningful word patterns can be formed by equidistant letter sequences: those formed by chance and those formed by design. First, there are coincidental or statistically meaningless word patterns, and second, there are deliberately coded word patterns hidden in a document for the purpose of conveying a message. In fact, the authors argue there are "hundreds, thousands and sometimes millions of ELS's that appear in every document in the world" which are "mere coincidences (until *proven* otherwise)." In other words, random or chance messages are commonplace.

Jesus Found in Other Books

Unfortunately, a great deal has been said in Christian articles, books, videos, documents on the internet, and lectures concerning the appearance of Yeshua (Jesus) in the Old Testament. The argument is that these ELS codes could not be the result of pure chance. In fact, this is just what they are. The odds are that Yeshua will "appear accidentally in the Torah [alone] over 600,000 times." "We searched the entire Torah for 'Yeshua.' Simplifying our search by limiting the skip distances to *up to only 850 letters* still yielded the word Yeshua over 10,000 times. (In reality, if one will search for "Yeshua" at skip distances of up to approximately 100,000 letters it will appear hundreds of thousands times.)"

The authors further point out that Yeshua can be found in other books:

> We searched for the word Yeshua in the Hebrew translation of *War and Peace*. The search was performed only on the first 78,064 letters, corresponding to the number of letters in Genesis. Since it is a *translation*, *all* its words and letters are, of course, not the original ones used by the author. Therefore, the translated text cannot possibly contain deliberate encodings of the word Yeshua. Yet, after again limiting our search to skip distances of up to only 850 letters, Yeshua appeared in this small portion of *War and Peace* 2,055 times. Searching the first 304,805 letters of *War and Peace*—the number of letters in the entire Torah— will yield Yeshua over ten thousand times, with skip distances of only up to 850 letters. If one will search *War and Peace* for Yeshua at skip distances of up to one hundred thousand letters it will appear *hundreds of thousands* of times.

Lenin, Krishna, and Moon as Messiahs?

Next, Rabbi Mechanic and his colleagues examined the claim of Christian writers that at the Messianic text of Daniel 9:25-27 the word "Yeshua" appears once at an interval of 26 (going backwards), which the Jewish authors note, is a significant number in Kabbalistic numerology. But, they say, this occurrence is meaningless as a suggestion that Jesus is the Messiah. Using the same method as the Christian authors, Mechanic and his fellow researchers found the name of the Communist leader Lenin encoded at the Kabbalistically significant distance of 49 in the same messianic text in Daniel. In fact, "Rev. Moon" is encoded in the same messianic passage four times, "*all going forward,* all completely *within* this passage, and all of them at *much smaller jumps* than Yeshua (3, 3, 16 and 20)!"

In other words, if a person argues that Yeshua (Jesus) is the Messiah because that name is present in "code" at Daniel 9:25-27, one could also argue that Sun Myung Moon or Vladimir Lenin was the Messiah because their names appear in code, too.

Thus, as for the general argument that Jesus must be the Messiah because "Yeshua" is found coded in hundreds of passages throughout the Bible, Mechanic and others state, "This is an extremely dangerous and irresponsible misuse of the authentic codes phenomenon." Using the same methodology, they found many other "messiahs," including "Krishna" and "Mohammed," in the same passages where Yeshua was found:

> Limiting our search of the Torah to skip distances of up to only 1,000 letters yielded the encoded words of Mohammed 2,328 times, and Krishna 104 times. Furthermore (David) "Koresh," the self-proclaimed messiah who was responsible for the deaths of over one hundred men, women and children, is found encoded in the Torah 2,729 times, at skip distances of up to only 1,000 letters. Searching for Mohammed,

Koresh, Krishna, etc., at *any* skip distance would yield their names hundreds of thousands of times. In fact Rev. Moon's name is found in the Torah at an ELS over 19 million times.

In conclusion, then, "Yeshua" is not deliberately encoded in the Bible, but is only a chance occurrence.

Christian authors also make the claim that the Hebrew phrase *Yeshua Shemi* (Yeshua is My Name) is found in chapter 53 of Isaiah. However, the same methodology reveals the phrase "Mohammed Shemi" encoded in the Torah 21 times.

Mohammed and Koresh as Atoning Saviors?

In the book of Leviticus the phrase "Dam Yeshua" (the blood of Yeshua) appears at a skip distance of the biblically significant number 7. However, the phrase "Dam Mohammed" (the blood of Mohammed) is also encoded in Leviticus, and 14 times in the Torah as a whole. Even the phrase "Dam Koresh" (the blood of Koresh) is encoded in the book of Leviticus, and ten times in the Torah. Buddha himself makes an appearance and is encoded in Genesis at jumps of 172 letters.

Jesus as a False Messiah?

The Jewish authors next point out that using the same methodology as the Christians, they can even "prove" that Jesus was a false Messiah. The derogatory word "Maysit" beginning with the 24,350th letter of Exodus, is encoded with "Yeshua" in Exodus at a skip distance of 172; "Yeshua" and "Maysit" are also encoded in Leviticus at a skip distance of 172, as is the encoded word "Mechashaif"—sorcerer. The phrase "Nabi Sheker" (false prophet) is encoded in Genesis five times at the same skip distance as "Yeshua." "In fact, the encoded words 'Yeshua' and 'false prophet' overlap twice."

They also documented how, using the same methodology, a person can "prove" that Jesus is a false prophet, a false messiah, and that Christianity is a false religion. Further, they found that Jesus is cursed by God, leads others astray, and is a liar. All this can be derived by using the same methodology that allegedly proves that Jesus is the Messiah. The authors of the article conclude:

> If this methodology is valid, then these counter "codes" should obligate [Christian writers] to accept their theological implications—especially since they were found using [their] method of codes research. This use of a "codes methodology" produces illogical, contradictory, and absurd results and are, therefore, meaningless. To publish books whose aim is to convince people that the Bible contains "Yeshua codes" that prove or confirm specific Christian beliefs, when, in fact, these "codes" are coincidental patterns, is dishonest. To promote a methodology that "proves" that Jesus is the Messiah, without revealing that the same methodology yields codes that "prove" *He is not* the Messiah, would be deceitful, were it deliberate.

The authors also stated:

> We have known for many years that there are critical codes—some of striking complexity—that present Jesus as a false prophet. They are substantially more sophisticated than the simple examples mentioned in Rambsel and Jeffrey's books. The unanimous consensus was, and remains, that these extractions are not valid codes because they will not withstand critical scrutiny, and, therefore, prove nothing. It would be dishonest and it would offend the sensitivities of others to use these *flawed results as an attack on their deeply held convictions.*

Improper Interpretation of Related Words

The authors then discussed other serious problems, including the impossibility of properly interpreting encoded words because a person cannot determine how they are properly related. *"The most important statement one can make regarding codes research is that it is impossible to interpret anything you find."* For example, finding the words "Yeshua," "Messiah," and "true prophet" deliberately encoded in close proximity in the Torah would prove nothing because those terms can be interpreted in completely contradictory ways. For example, is the one who originally encoded the message saying that Jesus is the Messiah and a true prophet? Or only that some people will think He is? Or that Jesus simply *thought* He was a true prophet and Messiah? In other words, even if we could scientifically prove that the alleged Yeshua codes were deliberately placed in the Torah, we haven't proven the theological teaching that Jesus is the Messiah.

> Therefore only words whose relationship conveys *objective facts* can be considered "related" words. For example, in the "famous rabbis" experiment, the relationship between the encoded words conveys a historical fact: a specific rabbi was born or died on a specific day. *The legitimate codes in the Torah can accomplish one thing and nothing else: They can validate the hypothesis that the author of the Torah is not human. Any statement or interpretation is inherently speculative.*

The Jewish authors then make a sad observation. In spite of the fact that the just-described use of the code has been proven "objectively, scientifically, and logically invalid," the response of Christians generally, they say, is to continue to maintain that the "Yeshua codes are genuine." Interestingly, the authors point out that Muslims now claim that *they* have "faith" that the "Mohammed codes" found in the Torah are genuine.

A Warning Against Careless Misrepresentation

The authors added that there are dozens of missionaries today who are using the "Jesus codes" in their efforts to evangelize Jews. These authors agree that theological debate over the Messiah is appropriate when voluntary, respectful, and based on agreed-upon standards of evidence. But they say that playing "letter games" with the Torah is tantamount to "misleading people with false evidential claims," and is unnecessarily offensive. The authors concluded their article as follows:

> We showed Rambsel and Jeffrey's statistical computations, including Rambsel's chapter on probabilities to a number of world-class statisticians and they were astonished—and some were appalled—at the utterly ridiculous claims. . . . They simply disregarded universally accepted scientific norms. There is not even one statistical claim or computation in their books that is normatically rigorous or true. . . . Yet, the only way that one can objectively demonstrate that a word pattern was deliberately encoded in a document, rather than it being an accidental appearance, is through an objective, scientific and statistical evaluation. Because this evaluation runs on extremely complex mathematical and statistical computations, the great majority of people are incapable of making this evaluation. . . . We therefore issue a challenge to Pastor Rambsel, Grant Jeffrey and all the other missionaries who are talking and writing about Yeshua "codes." Submit your findings to evaluation by unbiased experts. Convince a professional pure-mathematical or scientific journal to confirm that your "codes" are not mere coincidences. . . . (If not,) stop using your representations to impress people who are unfamiliar with the codes methodology, and are therefore, unable to provide their own critical assessment.

Then they said:

> Christian missionaries have written letters to the
> editors of many newspapers, produced videos, pub-
> lished numerous articles, appeared on television and
> radio, all falsely claiming or implying that their
> methodology is the same as the legitimate one, and
> that *Statistical Science* and world-renowned statisti-
> cians have confirmed that the "Yeshua codes" are
> valid. *Nothing could be further from the truth. These
> claims are false witness, pure and simple, and should be
> retracted publicly, widely and immediately.*[3]

We agree. So, this is one of our major concerns about the
Bible codes and their potential dangers—that for lack of a
more critical spirit, they will be used in unadvised and embarrassing ways. However well-intentioned these efforts may be,
they will bring disrepute on the very faith the proponents
had hoped to honor.

To be fair, however, similar charges can be leveled at some
of the lecturers for The Discovery Seminar. At one of their
presentations, Dr. Robert Morey heard Rabbi Mechanic,
Salomon, and/or Berger use the codes as an apologetic against
Christianity.[4] If so, they can hardly criticize Christians for mis-
using the codes "against" Judaism when they misuse them
against Christianity. Both parties are guilty. Dr. Satinover also
admits that certain other Jews fascinated by the codes "in fact
did misuse the codes to 'prove' that Jesus isn't the Messiah."[5]

The Danger of False Prophecies

Another concern is the fact that the codes, as used by
Drosnin, have given us unfulfilled prophecies—or more
bluntly, false prophecies. One such prophecy declared that
"Tokyo will be evacuated" as a result of the poison gas attack
of by the Aum Shinrikyo cult. Attempting to explain why
Tokyo was never evacuated, Drosnin commented that "'Tokyo
will be evacuated' was the unfulfilled prophecy, the probability that was prevented."[6] But how does he know that it was

only an unfulfilled prophecy prevented by human action, and that it was not an actual false prophecy?

The Consequences Could Be Serious

False prophecies should be of considerably greater concern when national heads of state or others in positions of governmental authority listen to them with the opportunity to act on them.[7]

For example, we need to be extremely cautious if we find a Bible code warning that World War III is drawing near. Drosnin, in fact, believed that he had found a Bible code that read "atomic holocaust" in 5756 (the Hebrew calendar for 1995–1996) and "holocaust of Israel" in that same year. Drosnin actually contacted General Jacob Amidror, the deputy chief of Israeli Intelligence, writing a letter of concern regarding the Bible code's prediction of an atomic holocaust. He wanted to show the letter to Prime Minister Peres. In 1996 Peres' senior military adviser, General Danny Yatom, called Drosnin in New York. "The Prime Minister read your letter, and he read your (earlier) letter to Rabin, [warning of the assassination]," said Yatom. "He wants to meet with you." A few pages later Drosnin recalls:

> On January 26, 1996, I met with Shimon Peres at the Prime Minister's office in Jerusalem, and warned him of the encoded atomic attack.... I gave Peres two computer printouts from the Bible code.... I told him that the odds of that [code] happening by chance were at least 1000 to 1.... "If the Bible code is right, Israel will be in danger for the rest of this century, for the next five years," I told the Prime Minister. "But this year may be critical." The source of the danger appeared to be Libya. I showed Peres that in the code "Libya" crossed "atomic holocaust." "I don't know if that means an attack will be launched from Libya, or from elsewhere by terrorists supported by Libya," I said. "My own guess is that Kaddafi will buy an

atomic device from one of the former Soviet repub-
lics, and that terrorists will use it against Israel."

Peres took it all in quietly.

It was clear that he had carefully read my letter to
him, and that he had not forgotten the [warning]
letter I sent Rabin a year before the assassination. . . .
He had only one thing on his mind, the stated danger
to Israel.[8]

The message apparently did affect Peres, who made a
public statement three days later in a speech in Jerusalem.[9]
Drosnin comments, "It was a clear re-statement of the warning
in the Bible code—that Kaddafi would buy an atomic device,
and that Libyan-backed terrorists would use it against Israel."[10]

Drosnin also got through to Prime Minister Netanyahu's
father, Ben-Zion, one of his son's closest advisors, with the
extremely disturbing message that his son would be killed
because the Bible code "predicted" it with the words "surely
he will be killed" crossing "Prime Minister Netanyahu."[11]
Associated words were "his soul was cut off" and "murdered."
As Drosnin said, "The code made it seem inevitable." Even
though Drosnin attempted to assure Netanyahu's father that
the message indicated only a probability and not a preordained fact, the "prophecy" itself hardly sounded so
doubtful.

Now it doesn't take much to see that predictions of this
kind can be extremely dangerous. We can imagine the results
that could have occurred if the Israeli officials had taken the
code's "warning" seriously and decided to act upon it. Their
actions could very well have led to war—a war that never
would have started if they had ignored the alleged proclama-
tion found in the Bible code. After all, the Middle East is a
powder keg waiting to explode; Israel has nuclear weapons,
and Muslim terrorists can get them all too easily.

What's important to observe is that the alleged prophecy warning of an atomic war involving Jerusalem never came to pass. Drosnin attempted to explain this by saying that the Bible code speaks of delays and the human responsibility to prevent things. Again, predictions of the future that are encoded with delays or that can be averted are hardly predictions that can be trusted.

> Three days before the date encoded with "holocaust of Israel," I met in New York with the Prime Minister's national security advisor, Dore Gold. The next day, I sent a final message to Mossad chief Danny Yatom, and General Yatom sent back word that Israeli Intelligence was on alert.

> But nothing happened on September 13, 1996. There was no atomic attack. The Hebrew year 5756 came and went and Israel and the world were still at peace.[12]

Drosnin then argued that the Bible code, indirectly, may actually have prevented World War III.[13] The code, of course, cannot tell us if this is the case, but it happily supplies several *other* possible dates for atomic war(s).

A Guessing Game

The examples we've just cited should demonstrate our point that endeavoring to follow the code can be a guessing game, even a dangerous one. What's more, Drosnin admits, "On several occasions we have seen things happen as predicted but not when predicted."[14] So are these genuine prophecies or not? What good is a prediction if it doesn't happen when the prediction declares it will happen? The obvious "rub," according to Drosnin, is a combination of human freedom to affect events, and the difficulty of properly interpreting the code. But if the author of the code was omniscient enough to predict specific events in detail, wouldn't he also be omniscient enough to predict all human actions as well?

Consider Drosnin's argument. The codes were placed by some advanced, omniscient intelligence to warn humanity about major catastrophic events such as great earthquakes, atomic holocausts, and so on. We have the freedom to either avoid or at least to prepare for these events.

So what happens if the code is incorrectly interpreted and we are warned of something that would never have happened in the first place? Would we know any different? What about the impact such codes might have over people's lives, or even whole nations, as it apparently did with Israel? How can we know if we can trust the codes so as to act on them when we don't have sufficient information to generate trust?

This problem was illustrated in an interview on the June 13, 1997 episode of "CBS This Morning." In the interview, Harold Gans and Michael Drosnin disagreed over each other's use of the code. The conversation related to the code's ability to predict the future:

Mr. Gans: "I'd rather be safe than say something which is inaccurate."

Mr. Drosnin: "Far better listening to the apparent warning than ignoring it."[15]

Gans is right and Drosnin is wrong. Any warning that is incapable of objective interpretation isn't even a valid *apparent* warning. It is far too dangerous to take chances, even if the warning concerns an event like World War III. Indeed, it's possible that the announcement of a warning itself could lead to a series of events that lead to a war. As Drosnin pointed out, World War I was itself initiated by a series of events begun by a chauffeur making a left turn instead of a right turn. This led directly to an assassination, and produced a series of events leading to the Great War. If a left turn could "start" World War I, then certainly something more complex and profound as the Bible code could prompt political decisions with serious ramifications. As reporter Byron Pitts commented on the controversies surrounding *The Bible Code,* "It's a battle of biblical proportions."

Speaking of battles, there are other sobering possibilities. Consider again the current tension between Israel and the Arab states. In the Torah, God declares the land of Palestine was given to the Jews, not the Arabs (Genesis 17:8). One can envision Muslims becoming not a little concerned about code research that actually proves or seems to prove that the Torah is divinely inspired, fueling Jewish claims. Already, according to Satinover, who is Jewish himself, "Jewish devotions to Torah [has been] turned into a flood" by the code's dramatic impact on Jews worldwide and in Israel.[16]

Muslims states, which have often claimed the land of Israel as their own, can hardly ignore a phenomenon that has the potential to turn great numbers of now-secular Jews back to religious devotion to the message of the Torah—a message which teaches that God gave about ten times more territory to Israel than she currently occupies. This includes most of Lebanon and Syria and about half of Iraq and Jordan. The Torah teaches that all this territory is destined, sooner or later, to fall into Jewish hands (Genesis 15:18-21; 17:8; Deuteronomy 34:1-4; *see also* Joshua 1:4).

The implications are significant. If code influence continues, one can only wonder whether Muslim states would see their hand being forced in an attempt to deal decisively with a problem before it becomes unmanageable. Satinover also wonders:

> At a time when the universal phenomenon of murderous religious intolerance had only just somewhat began to level, what would it mean if the most radically fundamentalist-seeming propositions apparently linked most tightly to but one faith were proven valid, using the most rigorous means of science? I

had already heard a number of rabbis opine that if the codes were valid, especially if they were, it would be best to hide them. It was far too late for that.[17]

The Danger of Occult Influences

Another concern is that possibly millions of people will become fascinated with potentially dangerous phenomena directly related to the codes, including numerology, divination, Kabbalism, and even Drosnin's suggestion that alien intelligences, not God, are the source behind the codes— opening up the realm of UFOs and strong associations to the occult.[18]

An Occult Origin?

A Connection to Kabbalism

Several articles about the Bible codes have noted that the initial idea for the code was derived from a Jewish form of mysticism/occultism known as Kabbalism, which is said to have possibly come to people through supernatural revelations.[19] Kabbalism was also heavily influenced by Jewish gnosticism and neoplatonism, and "resonates with magical practice and theurgy."[20] Collier's Encyclopedia describes Kabbalism in the following terms:

> The name is derived from the Hebrew verb kabel [to receive] and implies that the Cabala was received, in the form of special revelation, by a few of the elect, who were especially chosen for the privilege because of their saintliness. Those who received the esoteric doctrine in turn transmitted it likewise only to a select few capable of receiving and understanding the mystic lore and using it properly. Cabala is divided into two systems, the one theoretical and the other practical. Theoretical Cabala, which borders on dogmatic religion, consists of theosophical speculations and has for its principal thesis the idea that the world

is an emanation of the spiritual essence of God. . . . Practical Cabala deals with the theurgic (magic elements) in mystic esoteric doctrines. It is based on the belief that these doctrines can be translated into action, and specifically, that they can be applied for the performance of miracles and to speed the coming of the Messiah. It is concerned with the use, to achieve particular ends, of divine names and words, talismans, amulets, ascetic practices, and theosophic arithmetic. According to Cabala, angels may be conjured up by sainted Cabalists to do their bidding, and spirits and demons silenced by the use of prayer and amulets.[21]

Here we see that Kabbalism is comprised of occult doctrines and practices. Since it claims that its methods may be applied to "speed the coming of the Messiah," interest among Jews could be expected. And, although Kabbalists believe they may conjure up "angels" to do their bidding, and that they can deflect spirits and demons by prayer, this involves little more than the spiritual deception we find in many forms of the occult and mediumism. In such cases, former occultists report, the "angels" are in fact demons, who will also feign to be mischievous or evil spirits—all in order to deceive people. In other words, demons will imitate angels in order to trick people into believing that the "good spirits" they are dealing with are really divine beings or good entities.[22]

Now, the fact that something originated from occult sources does not necessarily make it false, but it certainly does make it suspect. As Dr. Satinover points out, "The claim that the codes existed in the Torah lay at the very heart of Kabbalah. . . . " yet he also refers to "the wild imaginings and unfettered abuses to which Kabbalah inevitably lent itself."[23] What are the implications if the concept of Bible codes *was* revealed from an occult source—especially one having a hidden agenda?

The Kabbalistic seeds of the Bible code can be discerned in the following on the Kabbalah discussion from the authoritative *Encyclopedia Judaica*:

> In essence, the Torah contains in a concentrated form all that was allowed to develop more expansively in the creation itself. Strictly speaking, the Torah does not so much mean anything specific, though it in fact means many different things, on many different levels as it articulates the universe of being. . . . The true essence of the Torah...is defined in the Kabbalah according to three basic principles: The Torah is the complete mystical Name of God; the Torah is a living organism; the divine Speech is infinitely significant, and no finite human speech can ever exhaust it. . . .
>
> To read the Torah "according to the Names" [i.e., the holy names of God possessing magical significance] . . . does not have any concrete meaning but rather one that is completely esoteric: far from having to do with historical narrations and commandments, the Torah thus read is solely concerned with concentrations of the divine power in various combinations of the letters of God's Holy Names. From the magical belief that the Torah was composed of God's Holy Names it was but a short step to the mystical belief that the entire Torah was in fact nothing else than the Great Name of God Himself. In it God expressed His Own Being insofar as this Being pertained to creation and insofar as it was able to manifest itself through creation. Thus, the divine Energy chose to articulate Itself in the form of the letters of the Torah as they express themselves in God's Name. . . . the single Torah appears in different forms in the different *Shemmitot* or cosmic cycles of creation. A direct consequence of this belief was the principle that the content of the Torah possessed infinite meaning, which revealed itself differently at different levels according to the capacity of its contemplator. . . . [thus] the

unfathomable profundity of the Divine Speech could not possibly be exhausted at one level alone, an axiom that applied as well to the concrete historical Torah revealed by God in the Theophany at Mount Sinai. . . . "many lights shine forth from each word and each letter," a view that was summed up in the well-known statement [itself an epigrammatic rendering of a passage in *Otiyyot de-Rabbi Akavi*] that the Torah has 77 faces.[24]

In other words, the letters of the Torah contain in concentrated form everything in the creation itself and when the Torah is mystically interpreted as the Divine Name/Essence, it may itself be considered an expression of the "divine essence." Its information content is infinite and capable of infinite meaning. It may thus reveal all that "was, is, or will be." Here we see the doctrine of the Gaon of Vilna.

Again, the fact that Kabbalists believed in and helped discover the code does not by itself prove the code wrong. But if the code itself is Kabbalistic doctrine, this raises certain questions that need addressing. If one fruit of serious code research is to endorse Kabbalism, occultism, and distorted biblical interpretation, then from a biblical perspective, this is hardly a positive outcome. The recurring relationship of the code to the Kabbalah (the Kabbalah is mentioned on 60 different pages in Satinover's book) shows that the potential exists for those fascinated with the Bible code to become fascinated by the Kabbalah. In fact, Satinover concludes that the Kabbalists not only helped lay the basis for discovery of the code, but also implies that Kabbalism per se is all to the good and even on the side of the divine. Not everyone is convinced, as chapter 9 reveals.

Given the divine prohibitions against all forms of the occult as found in the Old Testament (for example, Deuteronomy 18:9-12) and the prohibitions reinforced in the New Testament, what kind of association would be acceptable—in

God's mind—between the code and the Kabbalah? A series of questions needs to be raised, some of which we offer below:

If the code proves genuine, would God—or should Jews and Christians—use the Kabbalah to verify the divine nature of Scripture? Can the occult Kabbalah legitimately be blessed as an apologetic for biblical authority—even if the code ends up containing no specific divinatory messages but merely offers legitimate mathematical proof that God must exist?

But even such startling evidence as the Bible code will not convince people to believe in God against their will. Regardless—according to Romans chapter 1—people already know God exists because God has "made it plain" to them. On the other hand, if the code turns out to have divinatory messages, we run into some of the problems faced by Drosnin and others who promote a popular use of the codes.

Rips and Witztum believe that the code will be found to have an overarching message or messages (Satinover does not) but it will take years to determine whether this is the case.

> At least as it has been "decoded" so far, the Bible code seems to have no content at all—it is only a water-mark, a faintly visible seal of authenticity that must be looked at just so to be seen at all. (What makes it important, nonetheless, is the implication as to whose watermark it is.) Perhaps this "watermark" may prove to be the first indication of a truly lan-guagelike structure with a "message," as Rips and Witztum hypothesize. . . . however, I suspect that this is not the case. . . . As with [the legitimacy of some of the complexities of] quantum mechanics, only time and further investigation will tell.[25]

Again, what if the message(s) finally revealed by the code are unbiblical?

Perhaps we should ask whether there is at least the possi-bility that the code itself, legitimate or not, is a form of for-bidden knowledge? If "the secret things belong to the LORD

Our God, but the things revealed belong to us and our children forever"(Deuteronomy 29:29), then perhaps certain secret things should stay secret? Kabbalism of course, has as a central tenet the learning of the secrets of God and of the universe, which may be the very reason God warns against such mysticism. It may simply be too much for fallen creatures, or may lead to consequences which no one can now foresee.

As Satinover points out, the Kabbalists generally are reluctant to reveal the specific source of their revelations concerning the Bible code.[26] (At least one Christian heretic and Kabbalist, Trithemius of Spannheim, claimed he "was taught the art of codes in a dream.")[27] Kabbalists are also reluctant to reveal much about their occult practices. Yet they have made the occult a divine activity, baptizing it with God's blessing. Just as many people today mask the "supernatural reality" of the occult by defining it through the lenses of science and psychology, Kabbalists and indeed many other occultists today make the occult a godly, spiritual endeavor by how they interpret it. Thus, while the study of the occult for its own sake may be rejected, it is not rejected if a person first studies the Torah as a "safeguard" to subsequent study of the occult. The Gaon of Vilna himself did not oppose the occult; he simply believed that it was secondary in importance to the study of the Torah and that it could be pursued: "First learn the laws and commandments of the Torah, and fulfill them. For this alone is the Bread of life which satisfies man's obvious hunger. Only afterwards should you occupy yourself by the study of secrets. . . ."[28]

According to the *Encyclopaedia Judaica*, the Kabbalah has never been far removed from the occult, even among Kabbalists who warned against it. And even in Satinover's serious work, we find certain occult expressions: "There is no such thing as a single fixed reality—all phenomena and experience are unpredictable, fuzzy." . . . "To learn the template [of existence] is to make present both past and future; to study sacred history is to see the eternal in the mundane."[29] And:

One of the greatest of the later Kabbalists was Rabbi
Luzzatto, the Ramchal.... Describing the act of
"receiving" [the will of God], he comments:
"bestowed enlightenment" consists of an influence
granted by God by various particular means especially prepared for this purpose. When this influence
reaches a person's mind, certain information becomes
fixed in it.... And in this manner one can gain
knowledge . . . that could not be otherwise gained
through logic alone.... The main concept of
prophecy is . . . that a living person achieves an attach-
ment and bond with God.... The revelation of God's
glory is what initiates everything transmitted in a
prophetic vision. This is then transmitted to the
power of the imagination in the prophet's soul,
which in turn forms images of concepts forced upon
it by the power of the highest revelation.... certain
depictions were revealed to them [the Jews].... the
mysteries of God's divinity, as well as of His creation
and direction of the universe....

Thus, the "prophet" is the individual who, by the
manner of his life, positively binds himself to God. As
a consequence he becomes transformed into a suitable recipient for what God says.... The transmission
of information occurs via particular images stimu-
lated in the human imagination by the non-visualiz-
able dimensions of reality. The result in this instance
are more or less suitable "allegories" and "meta-
phors," the "more or less" reflecting the "level" of the
recipient, hence the "level" of "his" *inspiration*.[30]

In other words, the individual prophet, according to the
Kabbalist, is the one who has closest access to God and his
occult mysteries via mystical practices that illuminate the
mind and soul through divine revelation. To the Kabbalist,
anyone on the path could be God's prophet and partake in the
occult secrets of God and His creation. These beliefs cannot be

found in the plain text of the Bible but require "a mystical illumination" to be "seen" in the text. Another example of this mystical illumination is the Kabbalistic view that there are two biblical texts that form the foundation for the Kabbalah—one being the opening passage of Genesis, the other Ezekiel 1:15-16. But neither of these verses supports the Kabbalah—in any sense.[31]

It would be easy to conclude that if Kabbalism directly opposes biblical revelation, then the God of the Bible would have been unlikely to have used the Kabbalah as a means for revealing and even possibly "understanding" a code He had placed within the Bible (*see* chapter 9).

The Gaon of Vilna and Kabbalism

In chapter 2, we read that the Gaon of Vilna believed that the Torah included all the information that was or ever will be in the universe. How could he—and the Kabbalists—possibly arrive at such a conclusion? Did they receive it from some mystical occult sources? It would seem so. For example, the Gaon himself was a student of Kabbalism, and according to Mircea Eliades's *Encyclopedia of Religion* "had an exceptionally vivid visionary life."[32]

The following material illustrates how Kabbalists could easily have received information about the code form occult sources. It is taken from "Appendix F: The Mystic Life of the Gaon Elijah of Vilna," which appears in a book about another famous Kabbalist, *Joseph Karo: Lawyer and Mystic.* This excerpt shows involvement with mysticism, mystical revelations, "angels" and other "celestial beings," the dead, and out-of-body experiences. Although the Gaon clearly preferred study of the Torah to mystical revelations, there can be no doubt he was subject to strong occult influences (note especially paragraphs 3 and 4):

> The Kabbalistic writings of the Gaon Elijah alone
> exceed in volume those of all his Hasidic contempo-
> raries put together. . . . The Gaon Elijah was . . . an

outstanding talmudic and Kabbalistic scholar. . . . Elijah seems to have enjoyed mystical graces which, had he been a different man or lived in another century, might have made him the equal of Joseph Karo or even of Isaac Luria [due to his] Kabbalistic eminence and [the] "supernatural" life of the Gaon. . . . His most important disciple, Rabbi Hayyim of Volozhin (1749–1821), reports some interesting details of his master's life in his introduction to the Gaon's commentary on the *Sifra di-Seni'utha*, one of the obscurest parts of the *Zohar* (published posthumously, Vilna, 1820). There can be no doubt about the veracity of R. Hay's reports. The following paragraphs are extracts from his introduction. . . .

> Our great master, the Gaon and light of the world. . . . our pious and holy master and teacher Elijah of Vilna, from whom no mystery was hidden and who illumined our eyes with his holy writings in exoteric [halakhic] and esoteric [Kabbalistic] lore. . . . all the ways and paths of exoteric and esoteric wisdom were clear to him. . . . this is the gaon of the world. . . . he was granted to penetrate to the full understanding of all things. . . . I found myself obliged faithfully to proclaim to the tribes of Israel his complete and mighty mastery of the whole *Zohar*. . . . which he studied with the flame of the love and fear of the divine mystery. . . .

> Heaven wanted to deliver unto him supreme mysteries without any labour or effort (on his part) . . . through maggidim, masters of mysteries and princes of the Torah [i.e., different kinds of angels]. . . . I heard from his holy mouth that many times maggidim from heaven appeared to him, requesting to deliver unto him the mysteries of the Torah without any effort. . . .

> He experienced such ascents of the soul every night. . . . and one of his disciples confirmed to

> me that he had actually heard him admit this . . .
> [The Gaon is speaking:] "For last night [the
> prophet] Elijah visited me—if I remember rightly
> my informants did say that his name was Elijah,
> but possibly it was some other messenger from
> the celestial academy. . . . and revealed awesome
> things.". . .

To him these things were as "natural," and he did
not require any special meditations or *yihudim*. . . .
He used to say that God had created sleep to this end
only, that man should attain the insights that he
cannot attain, even after much labor and effort [in his
waking state], when the soul is joined to the body,
because the body is like a curtain dividing [man from
spiritual world]. But during sleep, when the soul is
out of the body and clothed in a supernatural gar-
ment. . . . one reveals to her [these insights]. . . .

Holy mysteries were revealed to him by the patriarch
Jacob and by [the prophet] Elijah. In other places
where he wrote in a general way that "it had been
revealed unto him." I am not quite sure whether these
were waking revelations or ascents of the soul to the
celestial academy during his sleep. There can be no
doubt that he certainly experienced ascents of the
soul every night. . . . as said before; but concerning the
revelations in his waking state, I have nothing certain
from him, for he kept these things secret. . . . To him
permission was granted. . . . to behold the inner
light . . . the most exalted and hidden mysteries . . .
and all the celestial gates were open to him. . . . [33]

Certainly the Gaon was well acquainted with occult phenomena, experiences, and revelations. So if the Gaon and
other Kabbalists did receive their theory from occult sources,
we must ask: Why was it revealed? Let's not forget—we do not
have to read far in the world of the occult to see its connections to spirits who, biblically, are said to have an undying

animosity for people generally, but especially Jesus, Jewish people, and Christians. It is possible, then, that the idea of a code revealed to get the Jewish mind off the plain message of the Torah, of which Jesus said, "If you do not believe his [Moses'] writings, how will you believe My words?" (John 5:47 NASB). Was it to get the Jews involved in all kinds of complex numerical "code" diversions? In part, could this still be true today for both Jews and Christians?

On the other hand, if the code is valid and the concept was derived from Kabbalism, then we have the unique phenomenon of what may basically be argued is an evil source of information (Kabbalistic occultism—*see* chapter 9) giving the world some of the most profound divine truths it has ever received. And yet those truths were not even hinted at in the plain teachings of the Bible.

A Revelation from the Spirit World?

Where did the Kabbalists get their belief system to begin with? Let's look again at what the Gaon said:

> The rule is that all that was, is, and will be to the end
> of time, is included in the Torah from the first word
> to the last word. And not merely in a general sense,
> but as to the details of every species and each one
> individually and details of details of everything that
> has happened to him from the day of his birth until
> his end.[34]

Dr. Satinover's translation from the introduction to the kabbalistic *Sifra Ditznuit* is even more specific:

> . . . the most minute details of everything that hap-
> pened to him from the day of his birth to the day of
> his death; likewise of every kind of animal and beast
> and living thing that exists, and of herbage, and of all
> that grows or is inert.[35]

Is God really sufficiently concerned enough about the "life" history of herbs and rocks that He would encode that information into the Bible? Again, how could anyone possibly have known that or even suspected it? The Kabbalists had no access to computers, and they would have found it impossible to devise a code manually. Given the occult nature of Kabbalism, we must at least consider the possibility that their insight could have been a revelation from the spirit world. Perhaps, in part, it was revealed to them for the same purpose for which this assumption is being used today—to divert people's attention from the plain meaning of the biblical text and to get them to spend their time and energy on supposed hidden codes and searching them out. We aren't saying this is the case, but that it could be based on the occult connection between Kabbalism and the codes, and the potential for code research to encourage diversions into the occult.

Of course, the Jewish individuals involved in code research are not necessarily being sidetracked from the biblical text because they are so heavily involved in Torah studies. However, if those studies are logically tainted by Kabbalistic hermeneutics, the net effect is the same or worse. Misinterpreting or even distorting the biblical text is hardly less consequential than ignoring it altogether—as cultic theology surely proves.

According to Drosnin, "Rips said that when he was working at his computer, searching for information in the code, he sometimes felt he was on-line with another intelligence."[36] Perhaps Rips' feeling was only imagined. But then again, maybe not. The interfacing of computers and spirits could soon be a reality, if not already. In their final impact Bible codes and computer programs alike can be manipulated by spirits, just as older divinatory tools were, such as the I Ching, tarot deck, runes, and of course, numerology.[37] The history of divination reveals that just about anything can become a divinatory tool. When employed as such, it sooner or later seems to attract the attention of spirits whose own actions, in the end, seem to prove them anything but divine[38] (*see* Acts 16:16-19).

If the Bible code proves genuine, Dr. Satinover is clearly correct that it "could signal the start of an age of combined scientific and spiritual exploration as has not been seen since the great sea journeys that ushered in the global society of the modern world."[39] But what kind of spiritual exploration will we see? What exactly will the codes point to? Again, we are faced with the "insights," biblical and other, relative to Kabbalism:

> The scientist will be driven to seek more than mere proof of the Bible code's reality and the validity of the Torah. He will want to understand the peculiar Kabbalistic probabilistic holographic and multidimensional structure of the code. An investigation into these features will inevitably raise analogies with quantum mechanics and to ancient Kabbalistic understandings. . . . because the Bible code itself emerged from [Kabbalistic] Jewish tradition—greater value than ever before will *inevitably* be placed on that tradition's ancient *interpretations of the Torah*.[40]

That is precisely the problem. The code originates from the Kabbalistic mysticism and its understanding of the Bible and therefore can *only* "validate" Kabbalistic interpretation of the biblical text. The difficulty is that Kabbalistic interpretation of the Bible is both incorrect and consequential. (*See* chapter 9).

It seems the case that most, if not all, of the Jews who have believed a code was hidden in the Torah have been kabbalists.[41] Rabbi Weissmandel's interest in the codes was inspired by thirteenth-century Jewish Kabbalist Rabbenu Bachya ben Asher of Saragossa, Spain, whose "teachings in Kabbalah . . . were highly respected at the time, and continue to be until today."[42] Rabbi Solomon ben Abraham Adret (1235–1310), Rabbenu's principal teacher, was also a Kabbalist who believed in the codes, along with Eleazer ben Judah of Worms (1165–1230), whose major work *Secret of Secrets* is also based in Kabbalism. Rabbi Abraham ben Abulifia, born in 1240, was also a Kabbalist. Rabbi Gikatalla and Rabbi Moses ben Nachman were also Kabbalists.[43]

In addition, it appears that many of the current code leaders are also believers in Kabbalism. Among them is Robert Heralick, a professor of electrical engineering at the University of Washington in Seattle. He is the author of over 400 scientific papers, and also an independent researcher into the Bible code who has assisted a prominent rabbi who wrote a book about it. "His observations about Kabbalah are especially astute and sensitive. They relate directly to the question of who would be able to receive and pass on such a thing."[44]

Kabbalists believe all knowledge can be found in the Torah by using Kabbalistic methods such as gematria, notarikon and temurah. If so, shouldn't all code enthusiasts and Christians especially, not to mention the general public, be more cautious about how they would use a phenomenon like the Bible code?

A critical review of Drosnin's book in *Business Week* commented on the problem inherent in different kinds of data mining: "The problem could get worse. With desktop computers becoming more powerful, data-mining tools are being used by people clueless about statistics. It's human nature to search for patterns—whether constellations in the stars or faces in the clouds. And computers allow that impulse to run wild."[45]

An example is provided of how data mining can lead to utterly false conclusions. David J. Leinweber, the managing director of First Quadrant Corporation in Pasadena, which manages some $20 billion in assets, sifted through a U.N. CD-ROM and discovered that historically "the single best predictor of the Standard & Poor's 500-stock index was butter production in Bangladesh."[46]

A Divination Tool?

The problem with "code bibliomancy"—divination by Bible codes—is that it can make people act in ways they ordinarily wouldn't have had they not received the secret information. What's more, divination is expressly forbidden in the Bible (Leviticus 19:26; Deuteronomy 18:10,14). With the Bible code's occult associations, there is no doubt the code is potentially divinatory. (It can contain *divine* predictions only if the code itself is *divine*.) If the code constitutes a *misuse* of the biblical text, then it can be *misused* as a form of divination. Certain proponents have said that the Bible code reveals the future. Whether that future is revealed by God, people's subjective code interpretations, false prophets, or occult sources makes all the difference in the world.

An Ever-Present Temptation

There is little doubt that people will be enticed to use the Bible code as a form of divination, which, of course, the Bible itself forbids. Even Rips acknowledges, "When the Bible code becomes widely known and *people try to use it to predict the future*, they should know it is complicated."[47] The fact that the Torah itself prohibits divination and that most—if not all—of the original researchers are Jewish people who presumably have respect for the Torah ought to be cause for concern. Apparently, even *they*, at least initially, became fascinated by the idea that perhaps there is a way to find predictions about the future.

In one of the end notes in Drosnin's book we read:

> Rips's colleague Witztum found *in advance* the precise date of the first Scud missile attack on Israel, 3 Shevat, 5751 (January 18, 1991). Rips confirmed that Witztum told him the date, and that Rips himself saw it encoded in the Bible, three weeks before the Gulf War started.[48]

What if the code soon reveals something similar to Israeli intelligence? It does not take much imagination to consider the possible outcome. There are now Jews—some in positions of leadership in Israeli government—who are beginning to believe or already believe the code constitutes a revelation from God. What if the leaders of a specific nation truly believe that one of the coded messages is a revelation from God that they are going to be attacked with nuclear missiles on a particular day—and that God has given them this revelation in order to save their nation? Wouldn't that lead them to carry out a preemptive first strike? Of course, if the code were wrong, a war would have been started for no reason at all.

Rips, Witztum, and Gans have all come out *against* using the Bible code for divination. They state emphatically that the code cannot and should not be used to predict the future.

> *Dr. Rips*—"All attempts to extract messages from Torah codes or to make predictions on them are futile and are of no value. This is not only my opinion but the opinion of every scientist who's been involved in serious codes research."[49]

> *Doron Witztum*—"It is impossible to use Torah codes to predict the future."[50]

> *Harold Gans*—"The book [by Drosnin] states that the codes in the Torah can be used to predict future events. This is absolutely unfounded."[51]

> *Michael Drosnin*—"I don't think the code makes predictions. I think it reveals probabilities."[52]

Yet even some of these individuals, initially, apparently used it in this manner, at least according to Drosnin. Drosnin's book cites conversations in which Rips and Witztum verify to Drosnin the genuineness of specific predictions.[53] If those leaders who warn so strongly against divination can be sidetracked, how much more can the general public become susceptible?

In his book, Drosnin indicates that the codes cannot be used to predict the future, because the future is only a set of probabilities. In a CNN Interactive World News story page dated June 4, 1997, Drosnin further stated, "None of us, neither Dr. Rips nor his colleagues, would claim to know the code well enough to understand it completely enough, that we can be certain what it says about the future."[54] Since the publication of his book and the initial criticism, Drosnin has come out more strongly against using the codes to predict the future. Yet, even though he says we are dealing only with probabilities, he still attempts to anticipate or predict the future. This illustrates how easy it is for people to become fascinated with divination, despite their own wise concerns.

Satinover also argues that the nature of the code prohibits using it for divination and finding personal messages. This does not address the issue of individual misuse of the code, but for some it may seem to answer the criticism that God could not be the Author of the code because of its divinatory potential. Concerning divination, Satinover states:

> In fact, the peculiar encoding method seems to preclude it: The code emerges only *when you find ELS's for two or more related facts that you have decided to look for*—an event and a date. If you know an event, but not its date, e.g., you may well find the event at some (minimum) skip, but what then? You can find innumerable arbitrarily selected dates in reasonably close proximity to any ELS. It is the fact that the *one* actual date appears surprisingly close to the event, surprisingly often, that constitutes the code. To be known to the person looking, the date must already be in *his* past.
>
> This distinctive [code] "boundary" on the phenomenon comports well with what the Torah itself says about fortune telling of any sort: without claiming that it is invariably impossible, the Torah states that it is strictly forbidden.[55]

Satinover reveals that during the Gulf War, the Israeli intelligence organization, the Mossad, and the military had created a list of three dates on which they thought that Saddam Hussein might attack. According to Satinover, in the code, "*all three* probable dates were in fact found in a compact configuration with other Gulf-related terms and *only* those dates."[56]

We can see that in the "fuzzy" nature of the code's "predictions," finding multiple predicted dates for events makes prediction useless. Satinover proceeds to argue as follows:

> If you know the name of someone, but not when he died, you couldn't search for his date of death to learn (that is, predict) it. You could search for all the dates within a certain compactness, and presume that his actual date may be one of these—but only probably. It is only *likely* that an actual name-date pair will be compact, not assured. Thus does the intrinsically statistical nature of the codes prevent them from them being used as an oracle. This finding also suggests something else: There are many possible dates on which someone might actually die, even though only one on which he does. If the analogy to the quantum nature of time is correct, then we would expect those dates to be spread out in a "probability" curve with some outcomes more likely than others. . . . And we therefore bump up against yet another "fence" that seems to have been placed with exquisite precision about the Bible code, circumscribing our potential to misuse it. We cannot use even startling individual findings to verify a matter. The code points to one thing and one thing only: the authorship of a document in which it is found.[57]

Thus, Satinover believes the Bible code "does not present the portrait of a wholly determined world known in advance but one in which many paths are possible, and in which our own choices are crucial."[58]

How do we respond to this? On the one hand, it does seem true that the code itself makes predicting the future difficult. On the other, human nature being what it is, people will try. Drosnin's book is proof enough and, certainly, he used the code in such a manner without much of a problem. So, the question is, in spite of the inherent difficulty, are there times when the code itself makes divination possible? And even if we believe the code cannot presently be used for divination, will an extension or modification of the code allow for this in the future? Then we must consider the fact that the code may contain an "escape clause" by how it clusters possible predictions. Satinover points out that of the three possible dates of the first Scud missile attack, the actual date on which the attack occurred was the one having the closest proximity:

> I have seen a document that states unequivocally that "that date"—the third of Shevat, the day that the first Scuds actually fell on Israel—was found *before* the war started. . . . That a number of potential dates (but not necessarily *all* potential dates) were identified in close proximity to the event and that one of them turned out to be the actual date, and happened also to be the closest of the three dates to the event, suggests an entirely different way of understanding how "time and chance happeneth."[59]

In other words, in the cluster of coded information, the actual date of the first Scud missile attack was closest in proximity to the coded event. This could be interpreted as a "key" of sorts to using the code as a divinatory method: proximity indicates probability.

Then again, as we saw, even Rips apparently conceded of the Bible code that people would try to use it to predict the future. He did not say it was impossible, but rather that it was complicated.

A Prohibition Against Divination

The following excerpt is from a chapter that critiqued divination from a biblical and scientific perspective:[60]

> ... divination for personal knowledge of the future is both unnecessary and dangerous. In Scripture, God has already told us the broad outlines of future history as it relates to biblical eschatology. His people are to trust in His Word and in His sovereignty in future events, both in their own lives and in the final outcome of human affairs. For very good reasons, God has not and does not reveal our specific, individual futures. For example, no one likes pain, and if we knew the future most of us would try to avoid unpleasant situations, suffering, and tragedy, which may, in fact, be God's will for us, thus avoiding what God has wisely determined is best for us from the eternal perspective.
>
> People grow in their faith and in their ability to endure things. God's will that cannot be endured at one point in life may be able to be endured or accepted at another. No one but God knows the final cost for not enduring His will (see Matthew 19:11-12; John 16:12). Had Jesus not accepted the suffering that was God's purpose for His life, what would have been the outcome? But how many of us would willingly face something like that were divination to reveal it? Only God knows what will finally be accomplished through the sacrifices and sufferings of His saints. This is why Scripture tells us, "Let those also who suffer according to the will of God entrust their souls to a faithful creator in doing what is right" (1Peter 4:19 NASB).
>
> Occult divination adopts an entirely different view, one that does not trust God for the future. By seeking to know future events, divination promises to allow the individual to control his future. In this sense, it

represents a fundamental rejection of God's infinite, wise, and perfect will, replacing it with the limited and self-serving perspective of the human will. Because it represents a conscious abdication of divine sovereignty for human "control," it is ultimately a confrontation with God. This is why the Bible strictly opposes divination. While it acknowledges that people use divination (e.g., Genesis 4:4-5), it condemns and never endorses such practices [Leviticus 19:26; Deuteronomy 18:10,14; 1 Samuel 15:23].

Clearly, if the God of the Bible prohibits divination, he cannot be the author of a Bible code that endorses it.

A Fear About Knowing the Future

On the June 11, 1997, episode of "The Oprah Winfrey Show," Drosnin further said, "I would never allow myself to be controlled by any kind of prediction or apparent prediction."[61] The difficulty is that his book reveals the opposite to be true. In cases involving important information, including the assassination of Prime Minister Rabin and the predicted atomic strike on Jerusalem, the predictions controlled Mr. Drosnin's actions quite noticeably.

That's the problem with divination. If the issues are serious enough, it can't help but affect our lives, and cause us to decide and act in ways we ordinarily would not. With divination, the issues are always serious by definition—they concern our future. That's exactly why divination *is* dangerous.

While Drosnin allowed certain predictions to control his actions, he also confesses that he will not look for his own name in the Bible code because he does not want to know his own future. Oprah Winfrey responded in a similar manner. When Drosnin was her guest and her television producers wanted Drosnin to look up her name, she said, "Don't look up my name and if you find my name, ignore the fact that you saw my name. Turn the page; go to the next page. Yea, yea I don't want to know either."[62]

The intuitive fear that Drosnin and Winfrey sensed here is exactly the reason why divination should be avoided. People who do look up their names and think they have found aspects of their future may end up hurting themselves by allowing their life to be controlled by mere speculations. But who among the easily influenced can long resist the temptation? After all, complete information about the future, down to the *smallest* detail, is said to be right there in the Bible code.

The Problem of Contradictions

Drosnin claims that the Bible itself predicts, in code, the existence of the Bible code within it. But does it make sense for a code within the Bible to contradict the Bible itself, encouraging people to use divination?

We find yet another contradiction, which is revealed in Drosnin's own words. He says, "The code seemed . . . to be from someone good but not all powerful, who wanted to warn us of a terrible danger so that we could prevent it ourselves. . . . [According to the Book of Revelation] the Bible is a warning of sudden and inevitable doom. But the real message of the Bible code is *just the opposite*. A warning is encoded in the Bible so that we can prevent the threatened Apocalypse."[63]

And, speaking of the Bible code, Drosnin adds, "It is not a promise of divine salvation. It is not a threat of inevitable doom. It is just information. The message of the Bible code is that we can save ourselves."[64]

How can the code be telling us the truth—that we can prevent the threatened Apocalypse in the book of Revelation—when the Bible itself, in the book of Revelation, makes it clear that Armageddon is inevitable? Does it make sense to trust a code that refutes the plain text of the Bible? And, how can we save ourselves? Have we been able to so far? To think that we can save ourselves—politically, spiritually, or in any other way—apart from God's help, is naive. If human history demonstrates anything, it is that we can't save ourselves.

Alien Intelligences and UFOs?

Drosnin opens the door to occult involvement through his belief that some alien intelligence is the source of the Bible code. He concludes his book by stating that "definitely we now know that we are not alone."[65] What or who exactly is our companion? Certainly, Drosnin does not think it is the biblical God. Even though he writes, "The Bible itself, of course, says that God is the Author," Drosnin does not believe it. He says, "I had proof there was a code, but not proof there was a God. If the Bible code came from an all-powerful God, he would not need to tell us the future. He could change it himself. The code seemed, instead, to be from someone good, but not all-powerful."[66]

In Exodus 32:16, we find a reference to the Ten Commandments. Drosnin believes that encoded in this verse is a hidden message: "it was made by computer."[67] Drosnin then discusses the alleged probability of other intelligent life in the universe having evolved, saying that such life may have evolved billions of years beyond us and therefore could be capable of encoding the Bible in such a sophisticated manner, as well as being able to do much more. He then suggests "that behind the 'miracles' of the Old Testament there was an advanced technology."[68] In other words, the miracles were actually the result of an alien supertechnology. He quotes Arthur C. Clarke: "Any sufficiently advanced technology is indistinguishable from magic."

With many UFO researchers, Drosnin goes from there to argue that the Bible is not divine revelation but is inspired by aliens: "We have forgotten that the Bible is our best known story of a close encounter. The long-awaited contact from another intelligence actually took place long ago. . . . The Bible code, is, in fact, an alternative form of contact scientists searching for intelligent life beyond this planet have suggested: 'the discovery of an alien artifact or message on or near Earth. . . .'"[69]

As we continue to read Drosnin's theory about the source of the code, it is easy to see how some people, upon reading his book, could become entranced by the whole concept of coded messages from a highly advanced civilization in outer space, leading to their personal involvement in mysticism, UFOs, and perhaps even contacteeism—which is actually a form of perilous mediumism, as we demonstrated earlier.[70]

Here's what Drosnin says:

> Physicist [Paul] Davies theorized that "alien artifact" might be "programmed to manifest itself only when civilization on earth crossed a certain threshold of advancement." That perfectly describes the Bible code. It had a time-lock, it could only be opened once computers had been invented.
>
> The rest of Davies' observation is again a precise description of the Bible code: "The artifact could then be interrogated directly, as with a modern interactive computer terminal, and a type of dialogue immediately established. Such a device—in effect an extraterrestrial time capsule—could store vast amounts of important information for us."
>
> Davies, winner of the Templeton Prize for science and religion, imagines "coming across the artifact on the moon or on Mars" or "discovering it suddenly on the Earth's surface, when the time is right."
>
> In fact, we have always had it. It is the best known book in the world. We have just never recognized what it really was. What Moses actually received on Mt. Sinai was an interactive database, which until now we could not fully access. The Bible that "God" dictated to Moses was really a computer program. . . . Now the computer program can be played back, and reveal the hidden truths about our past and our future.[71]

Here we have the Bible, the Word of God, reduced to a computer database programmed by aliens! This theme can be played out in a variety of ways not only to support the occult, but also to discredit the Bible.

When NBC host Matt Lauer asked Drosnin about who put the code in the Bible, he responded, "Presumably, the same intelligence that knew Yitzak Rabin would be the Prime Minister of Israel and that he'd be assassinated in 1995. In other words, some intelligence that could see the future."[72]

The difficulty with accepting this idea is that aliens, no matter how they "evolved," could never see the future omnisciently. Only God could have encoded the Bible with messages about future events because only God is omniscient. However, as a secularist and an atheist who does not believe in God, Drosnin resorts to believing in some form of advanced intelligence from a highly evolved civilization in outer space. Yet no matter how advanced an intelligence becomes, it would never be able to predict the future in the detail Drosnin presents in his book. Omniscience is required, and omniscience requires deity.

A Call to Caution

So what is our conclusion?

We have endeavored to follow the biblical admonition, "Examine everything carefully; hold fast to that which is good; abstain from every form of evil" (1 Thessalonians 5:21-22 NASB). We have noted some major difficulties in the whole concept of a Bible code. We've seen that the Bible is not the only text with seemingly hidden messages. Also, ancient Hebrew, with its many short words, lends itself to finding such messages. And, the Hebrew text Drosnin uses has the vowels present, whereas the original text of the Torah would not have had vowels.

We've found problems with some of the conclusions stated by those who discovered the Bible code, especially as presented in Drosnin's book. We've seen that not only is Jesus present in the Bible code, but also Mohammed, Krishna, and

Rev. Moon! And there are contradictions between the plain text of the Bible and what the codes are supposedly telling us.

For these reasons and others that we've presented, we believe it's necessary to refrain from being influenced by the Bible code or allowing it to shape our views of God, Christianity, our lives, and the future.

If there is a genuine Bible code, time will reveal it. Until then people, Christians and Jews especially, should be cautious.

8

Understanding the Kabbalah

The Kabbalah bears no small import to the Bible code. The principals most frequently associated with the code historically and today usually seem to believe in the Kabbalah. As we've seen in earlier chapters, the Kabbalah itself apparently was the original source for belief in the code.

What is the Kabbalah? The *Encyclopedia Judaica* defines it as "the traditional and most commonly used term for the esoteric teachings of Judaism and for Jewish mysticism, especially the forms which it assumed in the Middle Ages from the twelfth century onward."[1]

The standard *Encyclopedia of Religion* declares:

> Since the early thirteenth century it has become the main term for Jewish mystical traditions, which deal almost exclusively with [1] a theosophical understanding of God, combined with a symbolic view of reality and the theurgical conception of religious life, and [2] a way to attain a mystical experience of God through the invocation of divine names.[2]

The Kabbalist Worldview

According to the *Encyclopedia Britannica* the seeds of Kabbalism originate with the merkavah mysticism of first-century

Palestine, while *The Encyclopedia of Judaism* points out that Kabbalism represents a rebellion of sorts against traditional Judaism: "Ever since the second century CE, there has been a trend in Jewish culture which is not satisfied with traditional ways to approach God through Jewish religious practice and thought."[3] Instead, it seeks a more intimate and meaningful contact, and even union, with God.

Jewish mysticism, like Christian mysticism, strongly influences those who believe it. However, it does not necessarily influence the larger traditional theology of the religion itself, being outside it.

Kabbalism is divided into both philosophical and practical aspects, either of which would seriously alter an individual Kabbalist's view of traditional Judaism. Thankfully, not all Kabbalists accept the magical occult tradition of practical Kabbalah. But even these may still have engaged in mysticism or redefined occult practice into more acceptable psychological or "scientific" categories. Regardless, a true Kabbalist cannot help but be affected either by philosophical or practical Kabbalism, and frequently is affected by both.

This is the problem: Both philosophical and practical Kabbalism are opposed to the doctrine and commandments of the Torah and the rest of the Jewish scriptures. While modern-day Judaism has been more accepting of the Kabbalah, we think that nineteenth-century orthodox Jews correctly saw the Kabbalah as having a potentially disastrous impact on Judaism.

So that we can better understand the reason for concern over Kabbalism—especially in relation to the Bible code—let's take a look at its occult nature, its concept of God, and its approach to Bible interpretation. Although our analysis is brief, we have based our presentation on some key authoritative sources: The *Encyclopedia Judaica* (1972), Wigoder's *The Encyclopedia of Judaism* (1989), and Eliade's *The Encyclopedia of*

Religion (1987). We have also cited Ponce's theosophical text on the Kabbalah (1978) and Matt's text on the Zohar (1983).

The Kabbalah and Occultism

The most important work in the Kabbalah is the Zohar, a mystical "commentary" on the Pentateuch. Many Jews apparently view it as canonical, and after the Bible and the Talmud, it is the third most sacred book of Judaism.[4] Yet a standard theosophical text on the Zohar, *Zohar: The Book of Enlightenment*, suggests that the Zohar was in part the product of a human medium, and that it was written through automatic writing. This text describes the author as "an inspired scribe recording the wisdom of Kabbalah as it courses through him, a vessel channeling the Kabbalistic collective unconscious."[5] Matt further believes that "automatic writing would have contributed to" the Zohar's particular style, its foreign and invented languages, neologisms, reverse sequences of letters, and "strange conglomerations of words in otherwise clear sentences."[6]

Not unexpectedly, the *Encyclopedia Judaica* reports that various spiritistic methods are mentioned—for example, "Automatic writing is mentioned in a number of sources" and "A number of other spiritualistic phenomena, both spontaneous and deliberately induced, are also mentioned in various sources. . . . "[7]

As we've already noted, Kabbalism is divided into philosophical and practical aspects. Practical Kabbalah became so entwined with the occult—even black magic—that most Kabbalists disavowed it. Yet occult phenomena and practices are hardly infrequent in the life of Kabbalists. For example, Josef Karo and Shelomoh Ha-Levi Alkabets, two central Kabbalistic figures from Turkey, helped establish "mystical groups that formed the nuclei of intensive quabbalistic activities. Karo, the major halakhist of his time, produced a mystical diary dictated by a *maggid*, an angelic messenger who spoke from Karo's throat. Karo represents a Spanish quabbalistic trend that was primarily interested in incubational techniques to induce revelations and dreams."[8] Another of the dominant figures in Kabbalism is Isaac Luria, who was well known for his "occult powers, and exposition of a novel type of Theosophy."[9]

The *Encyclopedia Judaica* also discusses the occult nature of the Kabbalah in its lengthy article on the subject. For example, consider the following descriptions:

> From the beginning of its development, the Kabbalah embraced an esotericism closely akin to the spirit of Gnosticism, one which was not restricted to instruction in the mystical path but also included ideas of cosmology, angelology, and magic. Only later . . . the Kabbalah became a mystical Jewish theology. . . . This process brought about a separation of the mystical, speculative elements from the occult and especially the magical elements, a divergence that at times was quite distinct but was never total.[10]

And:

> For the most part, the realm of practical Kabbalah is that of purely motivated or "white" magic, especially as practiced through the medium of the sacred, esoteric names of God and the angels, a manipulation of which may affect the physical no less than the spiritual world. . . . only the most perfectly virtuous individuals are permitted to perform them [magical operations]. . . . Whoever else seeks to perform such acts does so at his own grave physical and spiritual peril. . . . [regardless] the boundary between physical magic and the purely "inward" magic of letter combinations and *kavvanot* was not always clear-cut and could easily be crossed in either direction.[11]

However, the *Encyclopedia Judaica* also points out that both black and white magic are practiced in Kabbalah and that, although the black magic is usually condemned, it hardly disappears entirely:

> The ostensible lines drawn by the Kabbalists to set the boundaries of permissible magic were frequently overstepped and obscured, with the consequent appearance in practical Kabbalah of a good deal of "black" magic—i.e. magic that was meant to harm others, or that employed "the unholy names" . . . of various dark, demonic powers, and magic used for personal gain. The open disavowal of practical Kabbalah by most Kabbalists . . . was for the most part in reaction to practices like these. Such black magic embraced a wide range of demonology and various forms of sorcery. . . . Such black magic is called in the Kabbalah "apocryphal science". . . . or the science of the Orientals . . . and, though a theoretical knowledge of it is permitted—several Kabbalistic books treat of it at length—its practice is strictly forbidden. . . .
>
> The opposition of the speculative Kabbalists to black magic was unable to present a conglomeration of all kinds of magical prescriptions in the literature of practical Kabbalah. Often the white-magical practices of amulets and protective charms could be found side by side with the invocation of demons, incantations, and formulas for private gain (e.g. magical shortcuts, the discovery of hidden treasure, impregnability in the face of one's enemies, etc.) and even sexual magic and necromancy.[12]

In essence, "what came to be considered practical Kabbalah constituted an agglomeration of all the magical practices that developed in Judaism from the Talmudic period through the Middle Ages."[13]

However, it is just such so-called "white" or "black" magical practices that are condemned in both testaments as a trafficking with evil spirits.[14]

Because the Kabbalah is hostile both philosophically and practically to biblical teaching, we should not be surprised to find that it endorses an unbiblical view of God.

The Kabbalistic Concept of God

The Kabbalistic concept of God is more Eastern than biblical. For example, as in *advaita* Vedanta Hinduism, Kabbalism divides God into two primary aspects, the one true unknowable God *(Ein Sof)*, and Its or His knowable manifestation (the *Sefirot)*. In Kabbalism *Ein Sof* "is inaccessible to thought and has no attributes."[15] The *Sefirot*

> are the manifestations of *Ein Sof,* Its mystical attributes. Here God thinks, feels, responds, and is affected by the human realm. He and She comprise the divine androgyne; the romantic and sexual relationship is one of the most striking features of the Zohar. Though ultimately God is infinite and indescribable, the *Sefirot* are real "from our perspective." They provide the human being with a way to know the unknowable.[16]

Again, similar to *advaita*—where we find *Nirguna Brahman* [Brahman without attributes], and *Saguna Brahman* [Brahman with attributes]—in the Kabbalah, we find the attempt to know the unknowable through its ultimately illusory manifestations.

Most relevant to Christian theology is that the Kabbalah teaches that the God of the Old Testament is an inferior deity to *Ein Sof.* Kabbalists say that because the biblical God has attributes, such as love, justice, and mercy, He cannot be considered the ultimate God, who is attributeless. We are told that in *Ein Sof,*

> all opposites exist in complete ignorance of their differences, in a unity beyond unity, which knows no possibility of differences. In the minds of the Kabbalists *Ein Sof* is no-thing, does not exist, is not

fathomable and cannot be discussed at all in terms of
Being or Non-Being. . . . The very most we can say is
that it exists in its non-existence, and that in its non-
existence it exists.[17]

Ein Sof is next described, with equal coherency, as a "spiritual non-entity" and "a plenum of emptiness." We are then
told, obviously, "the Ein Sof, by definition, cannot be com-
prehended. So he can be neither understood by what he is
not, nor by the idea of nothing. . . . "[18] Exactly who or what Ein
Sof is may be unclear to the unenlightened, but it or he is anything but the God of the Bible.

There is also no doubt that pantheistic, more so panentheistic, elements exist in the Kabbalah, although it cannot
broadly be classified as either. Some Kabbalists have argued
that "nothing is outside" the Ein Sof, while the Zohar itself
insists that God "is everything."[19] The difficulty is knowing the
"objective meaning" of such statements. In the context of a
mystical and subjective worldview, they could be interpreted
either theistically or pantheistically.[20]

When some Kabbalists declare that the emanated Sefirot is
"one in substance" with the Ein Sof, and that the human soul
"quite literally" is "a part of God above," the meaning
becomes clearer.[21] Cordovero, for example, is clearly one Kabbalist who held to panentheistic doctrine: "God is all that
exists, but not all that exists is God."[22]

Regardless, according to the Kabbalah, "Above all it is
important to understand that the Ein Sof of the Kabbalah
stands above the creator God of the Old Testament."[23] Para-
doxically, it is the God of Kabbalah, not the God of the Bible,
that allows himself to be manipulated in unseemly ways by
his creation. The techniques of mystical enlightenment used
in the Kabbalah allow the practitioner to "know" and even
manipulate God. They include recitation of the divine name,
meditation, various breathing techniques, and cathartic practices.

Some practices involve a meditation that empties the mind and is similar to Indian yoga and Muslim Sufism:

> [The Kabbalist is involved in] training in meditation. By immersing himself in various combinations of letters and names, the Kabbalist emptied his mind of all natural forms that might prevent his concentrating on divine matters. . . . The techniques of "prophetic Kabbalah" that were used to aid the ascent of the soul, such as breathing exercises, the repetition of divine names, and meditations on colors, bear a marked resemblance to those of both Indian yoga and Muslim Sufism.[24]

One of the goals of Kabbalah is to actually manipulate the divine nature. As Moshe Idel writes in *The Encyclopedia of Religion:*

> One of the most important tenets of mainstream Quabbalah is the view that man can influence the inner structure of the godhead. By performing the commandments with the proper Quabbalistic intention, man is capable of restoring the lost harmony between the lesser *Sefirot,* and Tif'eret Malkhut, making possible the transmission of the divine efflux from the higher *Sefirot* to our world. Moreover, man can draw this efflux from *Ein Sof,* the hidden divinity, downward to the *Sefirot.* . . . Quabbalistic observance of the commandments constitutes a theurgic [magical] activity, since its aim is the restructuring of God.[25]

It is thus significant that the manner in which the *Ein Sof* "created" the world parallels the occult practical methodology of "enlightenment" in dangerous Tantric kundalini yoga. Apparently, in imitating *Ein Sof's* method of creation, the Kabbalistic initiate mystically internalizes a similar process in order to "know" the means of creation within the body:

It is in the Kabbalistic system of Isaac Luria that we find an extremely intricate description of the activity of the *Ein Sof* in the universe prior to the creation. Luria tells us that the infinite being, *Ein Sof*, retreated from the arena of the universe, contracted into Himself, and left behind Him, in that space which was defined as Him, an emptiness. It was by the *Ein Sof's* retreat from infinite space into an infinitesimal monad of pure energy that the world comes into being. If the *Ein Sof* had not contracted Himself there would have been no space for the activity of Genesis to take place. The world comes into being only after this contraction. It was then that the *Ein Sof* sent forth a beam, an emanation of Himself into the space created by His contraction. It is on the "surface" of that space that the first spark was struck, the pinpoint of light which was to become the *Sefirot*.

In order for a creation to be possible there must first be a contraction, a concentration of all energies at a center. Then, an expansion must occur; the gathered energies must be sent forth in concentrated form as a ray or beam of energy.

The activity of the *Ein Sof* as outlined by Luria immediately brings to mind the method of yoga in which the yogin is called upon to retrieve the energies bound up with the sense-organs, dispersed in the world, and concentrate them on a center located in his body. In the Chinese yogic text called *The Secret of the Golden Flower* we are told that in order to create the flower, or subtle body, we must take the energies which normally flow outward into the world through the eye (i.e., the senses or general involvement with the world of the senses) and cause them to "flow backward." This withdrawal of energies might be likened to the *Ein Sof's* contraction of Himself.

Again, in the Tantric discipline of Kundalini yoga the purpose behind the retrieving of energies is awakening the bundle of spiritual energies slumbering at the base of the devotee's spine. After the initial contraction there is then a release of energies. But, as in most yogic systems, the newly found and released energy follows a specific path or course. So too does the expression of the *Ein Sof* after its contraction take on a course or series of paths.[26]

The Kabbalistic Approach to Biblical Interpretation

According to the *Encyclopedia Judaica, The Encyclopedia of Judaism,* and other sources, the historical approach of Kabbalism to biblical interpretation leaves much to be desired from the viewpoint of a normal interpretation of the text. Kabbalism may believe that the Bible is the font of all truth, but it also leans heavily upon a mystical interpretation of the Bible:

> Mystical truth . . . can be gleaned from a mystical interpretation of the ancient "biblical" texts. Throughout its history, Jewish mysticism has reflected the tension between the tendency to arrive at the mystical truth by an esoteric system, hermeneutical interpretation of biblical verses, and Talmudic sayings, viewing them as mystic symbols on the one hand and on the other, the drive towards original mystical discoveries, through visions, dreams, revelations of celestial [spirit or angelic] powers and intuitive reflection. . . . the Kabbalists saw themselves as transmitters of ancient secrets, given to them by previous generations or gleaned by them from ancient texts. . . . According to the Kabbalists these [biblical] words do not denote essential reality, but symbolize, in a complex way, a mystical truth which is essentially beyond words. God gave the mystics the Scriptures as a kind of dictionary of symbols which only the mystic can understand and in this way have some glimpse of the truth beyond these words. The mystics thus read the scriptures in a different, unique, way and they can use the symbols—the biblical terms—to express the mystical (truth) as glimpsed by them.[27]

In other words, the mystical truth of the biblical text is something that only the mystics themselves can discern through mystical practices. The plain meaning of the text is relegated to a secondary status. A classic example is the Zohar's hermeneutical commentary on the Pentateuch, which is anything but a grammatical-historical exposition of the text. Its "meaning" lies in the eye of the beholder.

In the *Encyclopedia Judaica* we are told that the plain meaning of the biblical text is inferior to the mystical interpretation of the Kabbalist. In fact, the author of the Zohar actually believed that if God intended the Torah to be a series of literal narratives, then he and his followers could have written a better text!

> In the main corpus of the Zohar, ... such mystical interpretations are referred to as "mysteries of the faith". ... i.e. exegesis based on esoteric beliefs. The author of the Zohar, whose belief in the primacy of Kabbalistic interpretation was extreme, actually expressed the opinion [3, 152a] that had the Torah simply been intended as a series of literal narratives he and his contemporaries would have been able to compose a better book![28]

To the Kabbalist, then, the biblical text is merely a symbol of higher truth and an inferior commentary on the true mystical text allegedly revealed by his fellow mystics:

> The Kabbalistic attitude to the Pentateuch, and in a somewhat lesser degree to the Bible as a whole, was a natural corollary to the overall Kabbalistic belief in the symbolic character of all earthly phenomena. ...
> The Torah became for the Kabbalist the object of an original mystical way of meditation. ... the true written law has become entirely invisible to human perception and is presently concealed in the White Parchment of the Torah Scroll, the black letters of which are nothing more than a commentary on this vanished text.[29]

Readers who focus on the surface meaning of the biblical text and its historical narrative are said to be harming themselves spiritually. The Kabbalist would say that the surface texts are simply the garments, and not the hidden inwardness that clothes itself in them. They say, "Woe is he who looks only at the garments!"[30]

Because the Torah has so many different interpretations, the conventional categories by which the Torah was interpreted—the literal, allegorical, biblical, and mystical—"served only as a general framework for a multiplicity of individual readings. . . ."[31]

With Kabbalistic hermeneutics, the possible number of interpretations of the Torah become endless: "From the sixteenth century on was expressed . . . the widespread belief that the number of possible readings of the Torah was equal to the number of the 600,000 children of Israel who were present at Mount Sinai—in other words, that each Jew approached the Torah by a path that he alone could follow."[32] Indeed, "The various possibilities of symbolic interpretation changed the scriptures into an 'open text' pregnant with infinite meanings."[33]

The *Encyclopedia Judaica* goes on to point out that the mystical meaning involved "the totality of possible Kabbalistic commentaries which interpreted the words of the Torah as references to events in the world of the *Sefirot* or to the relationship of this world of the biblical heroes" and therefore the literal interpretation was only the Torah's outermost aspect— the "husk that first met the eye of the reader" and had to be "peeled off" in order to find the true kernels of truth:

> As a result, the other layers revealed themselves to that more penetrating and latitudinous power of insight which was able to discover in the Torah general truths that were in no way dependent on their immediate literal context. Only on the [mystical] level of *sod* did the Torah become a body of mystical symbols which unveiled the hidden life-processes of the Godhead and their connections with human life.[34]

Unfortunately, as we saw in chapter 3, if we resort to mystical and subjective interpretations, then the Bible can be made to teach *anything!* Far from respecting the biblical text, mystical and subjective approaches undermine it.

One example of the problem with resorting to mystical interpretations can be found in Satinover's book, where he cites the Kabbalistic interpretation of Genesis. Citing Kabbalist Nechunya ben HaKanah, he writes, "In his view, the universe is not a mere few thousand years old as the text seems to claim on the surface, but is 15.3 billion years old, the very age arrived at only recently by estimates of modern astrophysical theories of 'big bang.'"[35] The problem is that the big bang theory is, in all probability, incorrect—and it is impossible scientifically to declare whether or not the universe is young or old.[36]

We have seen that according to Kabbalism, the ultimate God of Kabbalah is superior to the God of the Bible. If we attempt to understand the Bible by reading the text in a normal, literal fashion, then we will end up with an inferior understanding of God, revelation, salvation, reality and so on, because we will have sacrificed the underlying mystical truths of Scripture.

Kabbalists would say that literal interpretation is not necessarily wrong, only that it is inferior and incomplete. They say there is a higher dimension to knowing God than what we find in the literal text of the Torah.

We are therefore told that the mystical truth of the Torah is superior to its literal and superficial meaning: "The Zohar never loses sight of its goal: the creation of a mystical commentary on the Torah. . . . Through commentary, midrash and mystical hermeneutics, the Zohar introduces the reader to this hidden dimension of Torah. . . . The literal text is the starting point but the Zohar is dissatisfied with the superficial meaning"—and even irreverent towards it![37] Overall, "the Zohar may abandon the literal sense of a verse or, conversely, employ the technique of mystical literalness, reading hyper-literally. The goal is to penetrate, to unlock the secret content of the word, to elicit its divine essence."[38]

Indeed, even the letters of the Torah itself, used mystically, are said to have mystical powers: "not only does the Torah come from God; her words and letters are permeated with God" hence they are believed to have mystical powers.[39]

The purpose of the Kabbalah, then, is "to broaden the dimensions of the Torah and to transform it from the law of the people of Israel into the inner secret law of the universe. . . . "[40] One wonders: What does the God who gave the law to Israel think of such an endeavor?

Approaching the Torah in a mystical manner is believed to convey great benefit:

> Studying and living [the] Torah are the surest ways to
> a direct encounter with God. . . . [But] Torah is not
> merely law; it is cosmic law, a blueprint of creation.
> The Zohar illuminates the cosmic aspect of Torah. It
> strengthens tradition and at the same time transforms
> it. The literal sense is sanctified but readers are urged
> to 'look under the garment of Torah.' . . . [where]
> Theosophy replaces theology.[41]

Thus we are told by Kabbalist Moses Cordovero that "those who constantly create new interpretations [of the Torah] are harvesting Her"—that is, God's creative power.[42]

However, the Kabbalist approach to biblical interpretation consistently nullifies the plain meaning of the text. What, then, is the sense of even having the plain text of the Bible? When we compare the two, we see that the plain text is remarkably consistent and cohesive, whereas the Kabbalist interpretations are contradictory and clearly subjective. Whether these "doctrines" can supply the Kabbalist with what he or she needs in life, not to mention what God will require of them, remains to be seen.

Finally, it must be said that not all Kabbalists are prone to occult philosophy, practice, and hermeneutics:

> This type of Quabbalah commonly mitigated or totally nullified the mythical elements that are paramount in mainstream Quabbalah, including the theurgical nature of the commandments, processes by which God's internal life unfolds, and Messianic eschatology. For this reason, representatives of philosophical Quabbalah never became influential in Jewish theology.[43]

The Kabbalist Influence

It also remains to be seen just where Bible code Kabbalists lie in their use of the Kabbalah and how their views influence their view of God and scripture. We have been told by serious Christian code researchers that "general code research has nothing to do with Kabbalism," which in its good sense is "meant as a teaching tool and nothing more." That also remains to be seen. Whatever the outcome, it is difficult to deny the significant influences Kabbalism has had on Judaism historically, as the following extended excerpt from the *Encyclopedia Judaica* reveals:

> The influence of the Kabbalah has been great, for it has been one of the most powerful forces ever to affect the inner development of Judaism, both horizontally and in depth. Jewish historians of the nineteenth century, while conceding the Kabbalah's significant role, considered it to have been overwhelmingly negative and even catastrophic, but the appraisal of twentieth-century Jewish historiography has been far more positive. . . .
>
> As was pointed out. . . . the Kabbalah represented a theological attempt, open to only a relative few, whose object was to find room for an essentially mystical world-outlook within the framework of traditional

Judaism without altering the latter's fundamental principles and behavioral norms. To what extent if at all this attempt was successful remains open to debate but there can be no doubt that it achieved one very important result, namely, that for the three-hundred-year period roughly from 1500 to 1800 (at the most conservative estimate) the Kabbalah was widely considered to be *the* true Jewish theology, compared with which all other approaches were able at best to lead an isolated and attenuated existence. . . .

The main influence of Kabbalah on Jewish life must be sought in the three areas of prayer, custom and ethics. Here the Kabbalah had practically unlimited freedom to exert its influence. . . .

Many Kabbalistic concepts were absorbed at the level of folk beliefs, such as the doctrine of man's first sin as the cause of a disruption in the upper worlds, the belief in transmigration of souls, the Kabbalistic teachings about the Messiah, or the demonology of the latter Kabbalah. Throughout the Diaspora, the number of folk customs whose origins were Kabbalistic was enormous; many were taken directly from the Zohar, and many others from Lurianic tradition. . . . Such customs came on the whole to fulfill four mystical functions: the establishment of a harmony between the restrictive forces of *Din* and the outgoing forces of *Rahamim*; to bring about or to symbolize the mystical "sacred marriage" between God and His *Shekinah*; the redemption of the *Shekinah* from its exile amid the forces of the *sitra ahra*; the protection of oneself against the forces of the *sitra ahra* and the battle to overcome them. Human action on earth assists or arouses events in the upper worlds, an interplay that has both its symbolic and its magical side. Indeed, in this conception of religious ceremony as a vehicle for the workings of divine forces, a very

real danger existed that an essentially mystical perspective might be transformed in practice into an
essentially magical one. . . .

This penetration of Kabbalistic customs and beliefs
left no corner of Jewish life untouched.[44]

The question for Kabbalists, Judaism, and the Bible code
is whether such influence was ever justified in the first place.

9

The Clear Message of the Bible

Proponents of the Bible code believe it will prove to be of immense importance. Skeptics, on the other hand, speak of immense deception.

Whatever the outcome, we believe it would be unwise for those interested in this phenomenon, regardless of their secular or religious persuasion, to allow it to shape their views of the Bible. If the Bible code proves false, then in the minds of many people, right or wrong, the Bible itself will suffer defeat. If it proves true, it is hard to see how Kabbalism itself would not also be justified and energized. The truth is that for 3,000 years, the Bible has stood quite well on its own.

Even many skeptics of the Old and New Testaments agree that they are among most important and influential works of human history. Dr. Michael Shermer, the publisher of *Skeptic* magazine, the director of the Skeptic Society, and an instructor in science and in the history of ideas at several California colleges and universities, remarks that the "Bible is one of the greatest works of literature in the history of Western thought. . . . Few works have been so influential to so many people for so many millennia."[1] Indeed, based on its influence upon the world, the Bible may safely be considered the most significant book that ever was. It has become the most translated, memorized, purchased, loved, hated, prophetic, and evidentially verified book in the world.

Only the fact that the Bible's content and power are unique can explain the comments we cite below. Certainly, given its content, there is no other volume like it found anywhere in the world. Let's look at a few examples of what some of the most informed and famous individuals have stated about its uniqueness, influence, and practicality.[2] We offer these comments so that some sense of biblical influence historically can be gauged and also that readers might perhaps come to appreciate anew a truly remarkable book.

Patrick Henry declared the Bible "is a book worth all the other books that were ever printed." Abraham Lincoln commented that, "This great book . . . is the best gift God has given to man. . . ." Charles Dickens was convinced that "the New Testament is the best book the world has ever known or will know." William Gladstone believed that "the Bible was stamped with specialty of Origin and an immeasurable distance separates it from all competitors." Robert E. Lee wrote that "the Bible is a book in comparison with which all others in my eyes are of minor importance. . . ." Jean Jacques Rousseau declared, "I must confess to you that the majesty of the Scriptures astonishes me. . . ." Finally, Blanche Mary Kelly argued that "the Bible is the most stupendous book, the most sublime literature, even apart from its sacred Character, in the history of the world."

Indeed, the most ardent atheist is unable to logically deny the unparalleled influence of the Bible in our world. Ulysses Grant stated, "To the influence of this book, we are indebted for all the progress made in true civilization, and to this book we must look as our Guide in the future." In a similar manner William Lyon Phelps argued correctly that the Bible has influenced each of our lives more than most of us are aware: "Western civilization is founded upon the Bible; all our ideas, our wisdom, our philosophy, our literature, our art, our ideals, come more from the Bible than all other books put together."

Samuel Taylor Coleridge wrote that "for more than a thousand years, the Bible, collectively taken, has gone hand in hand with civilization, science, law—in short, the moral and intellectual cultivation of the species always supporting and leading the way." E.S. Bates concluded, "No individual, no Caesar or Napoleon, have had such a part in the world's history as this book."

It is somewhat surprising that not only are most people unaware of the Bible's influence, but they are also unaware of its potential to profoundly affect their own lives, the lives of their children, and the life of their country and culture. It can hardly be denied that a nation that honors the moral and ethical teachings of the Bible will be a nation that possesses understanding, compassion, love, and wisdom. Thomas Jefferson was correct when he said that "the studious perusal of the sacred volume make better citizens, better fathers and better husbands." I. Friedlander wrote that the Bible "called into being a system of morality which has become the cornerstone of human civilization." President Woodrow Wilson argued that "a man has found himself when he has found his relation to the rest of the universe, and here is the book in which those relations are set forth."

Those who have reverently studied and learned the Bible are unanimous that its power is transforming. It is perpetually relevant, always encouraging us to live better lives. It consoles our pain and imparts wisdom whenever needed. Cecil B. deMille declared, "After more than 60 years of almost daily reading of the Bible, I never fail to find it always new and marvelously in tune with the needs of every day." Johann Wolfgang von Goethe believed that "the Bible grows more beautiful as we grow in our understanding of it." Immanuel Kant stated, "The Bible is the greatest benefit which the human race has ever experienced," and "a single line in the Bible has consoled me more than all the books I ever read besides." Isaac Newton remarked, "I account to the Scriptures of God the most sublime philosophy." Roger Bacon concluded, "There is one wisdom which is perfect, and this is contained in the Scriptures."

Perhaps this was the reason A.M. Sullivan wrote, "The cynic who ignores, ridicules, or denies the Bible, spurning its spiritual rewards and aesthetic excitement, contributes to his own moral anemia."

That's only a small sampling of people's beliefs concerning the Bible's relevance. Given such accolades, is there any reason we shouldn't want to become better informed biblically? A good case can be made that the biblical illiteracy of our age plays a major role in the tremendous social, moral, political, and cultural problems we have faced in the last generation.

Rather than look to a hidden Bible code, the message of which is unclear, we believe that our readers and even our nation's interests are better served by looking to the plain message of the Bible itself in its high moral and spiritual teachings—and to a personal, triune, infinite God who declares He loves mankind, who incarnated Himself in the Person of Jesus Christ to prove it, and who brings meaning and significance to this life and the beyond:

> This is eternal life: that they may know you, the only
> true God, and Jesus Christ, whom you have sent
> (John 17:3).

Galileo wrote, "I believe that the intention of Holy Writ was to persuade men of the truths necessary to salvation." One of those truths is the oft-quoted declaration of Jesus Christ Himself in John 3:16: "For God so loved the world that he gave his one and only Son, that whoever believes in him shall not perish but have eternal life."[3]

Notes

Note to the Reader:
The endnotes referenced "Internet" were taken from the standard web search engines under the topics "The Bible Code," "Official Torah Codes," and so on. These sites did not always contain page numbers. The search engines used include Yahoo, Lycos, Pathfinder, Electric Library, Simon and Schuster Website, and CNN Interactive.

All transcripts were purchased from Burrell's Information Services, P.O. Box 7, Livingston, NJ 07039 (1-800-777-TEXT).

Doron Witztum, Eliyahu Rips, and Yoav Rosenberg, "Equidistant Letter Sequences in the Book of Genesis," *Statistical Science*, 1994, vol. 9, no. 3, pp. 429-38 is available in full from The Institute of Mathematical Statistics, 3401 Investment Blvd., Ste. 7, Hayward, CA 94545 ($20) or in abridged form at *http://www.fortunecity.com/tattooine/delany/11/genesis.html*

The comments of Robert Kass, editor of *Statistical Science*, are at *http://www.fortunecity.com/tattooine/delany/11*

Dror Bar-Natan, Alec Gindis, Aryeh Levitan, Brendan McKay, "Report on new ELS tests of Torah," published at: *http://www.math.gatech.edu/~jkatz/Religions/Numerics/report.html*

A CNN interview, "Meet Michael Drosnin," is at: *http://www.cnn.com/WORLD/9706/04israel.bible/drosninlog.html*

Doron Witztum, Eliyahu Rips, and Yoav Rosenberg, "Hidden Bible Codes Researchers Condemn Michael Drosnin," Press release issued 1997-JUN-4, is available at: *http://www.discoveryseminar.org/cgibin/var/aishdisc/press.html*

Doron Witztum issued a public statement June 4, 1997, which is available at: *http://www.discoveryseminar.org/cgibin/var/aishdisc/witztum.html*

Harold Gans, "Public statement," 1997-JUN-3, is available at: *http://www.fortunecity.com/tatooine/delany/11/public2.html*

The Yahoo search engine maintains a section on Torah codes at: *http://www.yahoo.com/SocietyandCulture/Religion/FaithsandPractices/Judaism/Teachings/Torah/T*

Chapter 1 — Introducing the Bible Code

1. Michael Drosnin, *The Bible Code* (New York: Simon & Schuster, 1997), p. 21.
2. Michael Drosnin, interview on "Today," May 29, 1997, transcript p.13.
3. Drosnin, p. 46.
4. Ibid., p. 26.
5. Ibid.
6. Jeffrey B. Satinover, *Cracking the Bible Code* (New York: William Morrow & Co., 1997), p. 121.
7. Ibid., back cover.
8. Ibid., pp. 1, 14-15.
9. Ibid., p. 20.
10. Ibid., p. 144.
11. As cited in Satinover, p. 146, quoting Dr. Michelson, "Codes in the Torah," B'OrHaTorah no. 6, 1987, pp. 37-39.
12. Satinover, p. 152.
13. Ibid., p. 154.
14. Ibid., pp. 163-64.
15. Ibid., p. 164.
16. Ibid., pp. 165-67.
17. Ibid., pp. 177-78.
18. Ibid., pp. 184-86.
19. David Van Biema with reporting by Lisa McLoughlin, "Deciphering God's Plan," *Time*, June 9, 1997, Internet copy.
20. Cathy Lynn Grossman, "Critics Say 'Bible Codes Predictions Don't Add Up,' " *USA Today*, June 4, 1997, p. 8d.

Chapter 2 — The Research Behind the Code

1. Public statement by Doron Witztum, "Official Torah Codes," June 4, 1997, Internet document.
2. Doron Witztum, Eliyahu Rips, Yoav Rosenberg, "Equidistant Letter Sequences of Genesis," *Statistical Science*, vol. 9, no. 3, 1994.
3. Public statement by Doron Witztum, Internet document.
4. Jeffrey B. Satinover, *Cracking the Bible Code* (New York: William Morrow & Co., 1997), pp. 5, 24, 33, 69-72.
5. Doron Witztum, et al., p.429, 433; cf. Satinover, p. 203.
6. Jeffrey B. Satinover, "Divine Authorship?" "Computer Reveals Startling Word Patterns," *Bible Review*, October 1995, Internet copy.
7. Jeffrey B. Satinover, *Cracking the Bible Code* (New York: William Morrow & Co., 1997), p. 203.
8. Ibid. In *Cracking the Bible Code,* Satinover reports this was a carefully crafted piece reporting on a small portion of their work previously published in Hebrew in the *Journal of the Israel Academy of Sciences.*
9. Public statement by Doron Witztum, Internet document.
10. Doron Witztum, Eliyahu Rips, Yoav Rosenberg, "Equidistant Letter Sequences of Genesis," *Statistical Science*, vol. 9, no. 3, 1994, Prefatory note by Robert E. Kass.
11. Satinover, "Divine Authorship?"
12. Drosnin, p. 192.
13. Satinover, "Divine Authorship?"
14. Drosnin, p. 23.
15. Ibid.
16. Public statement by Harold Gans, "Official Torah Codes," June 3, 1997, Internet document. Dr. Robert Morey cites Gans as stating, "I had already been convinced of the code's validity before the experiment," suggesting some confusion between Drosnin's account or Gans'

memory (or the sequence of events between the 1988 and 1994 articles) and possibly causing some doubt as to the objective nature of his research. (Robert Morey, *Biblical Numerics: Fact or Fantasy* (Newport, PA: Truth Seekers, 1997 ms. copy).

On the other hand, Gans' research seems solid, e.g.,:

> Gans has recently completed a paper entitled "Coincidence of Equidistant Letter Sequence Pairs in the Book of Genesis." In this paper, he repeats the original Witztum, Rips, and Rosenberg compactness measure, but assesses its statistical significance using a different technique. The results, he reports, are at a "significance level of 7×10^{-6} ($p < 0.000007 = 1/143,000$)."

Gans then took the names of *all* 66 Great Sages from both the first list of 34 individuals and the second list of 32. He paired all 66 names with their *cities* of birth and/or death, the spellings of those cities being searched out—as in the original Witztum, Rips, and Rosenberg experiment with their dates of death and/or birth—at minimum or near-minimum equidistant letter intervals. This kind of experiment could accomplish two things. First Gans was de facto testing the reality of the phenomenon on the first list of Great Sages (which results were not reported in the *Statistical Science* article as protection against "tuning and snooping"). But, second, for this approach to validate the Bible Code—*it would have to work with a whole new set of historical pairings:* the cities as well. The results were startling: They were significant at a level of $p < 0.000005$; that is, less than $1/200,000$.

These results are especially striking when you consider that in the original experiment, the "internal" control was the elegant randomization procedure suggested by [Persi] Dianconis: The rabbis' names were matched up with 999,999 different sets of wrong dates. Think of those dates as simply strings of letters. With these "wrong" strings the phenomenon was utterly erased. Surely if there was an underlying flaw in the procedure, or if the phenomenon was due to inadvertent tinkering over the years in which the compactness measure was "fitted" to *those* particular data (or vice versa, or both)—or if the codes themselves simply do not really exist—then matching the rabbis' names with a different set of letter strings (the cities) should have produced results nearly identical to the mismatched names and dates.

Gans has submitted his paper to a number of journals. He has been told that, on the one hand, the mathematics is perfectly in order, but on the other, "nobody is interested." Yet many expert critics have suggested that not only would a critique by a cryptologist be in order as a reasonable next step, but what would now be publishable were replications of the phenomenon, and extensions, using different data.

My guess is that replicating and extending studies on the codes will not be published until someone publishes a worthy critique of the original Witztum, Rips and Rosenberg paper. With that, precisely because of the code of honor among scientists, the door will be open for the kind of free exchange of ideas that alone will reveal whether the Bible code is a chimera—or the most astounding scientific research ever. (Jeffrey B. Satinover, *Cracking the Bible Code*, pp. 224-25).

17. Satinover, p. 223.
18. Drosnin, pp. 23-24.
19. Jeffrey Satinover, response in *Bible Review*, November 1995, cited by Grant R. Jeffrey, *The Signature of God*, (Wheaton, IL: Tyndale, 1997), p. 215.
20. Drosnin, p. 44.
21. Ibid, p. 43.
22. Ibid.

23. Ibid.
24. Ibid., p. 92. *See* Satinover, "Technical Appendix C," and pp. 262-63, 329.
25. Witztum, et al., p. 430.
26. Shlomo Sternberg, "Snake Oil for Sale," *Bible Review,* August 1997, p. 25.
27. Bruce David Wilner, "An Impartial opinion of the 'Torah Codes," Internet document.
28. Satinover, "Divine Authorship?"
29. Eliyahu Rips, "Preliminary Analysis and Comments on the Report of the New ELS Tests of Dror Bar-Natan, Alec Gindis, Arieh Levitan and Brendan McKay," Internet document.
30. Van Biema, "Deciphering God's Plan," cf. Benjamin Wittes, "Cracking God's Code: Maybe the Lord *did* write the Bible," Internet copy; this may refer to the paper critiqued by Rips.
31. Drosnin, p. 190.
32. Satinover, p. 262-63.
33. Wittes, "Cracking God's Code: Maybe the Lord *did* write the Bible," Internet copy.
34. Satinover, p. 225, 320.
35. Ibid., p. 225.

Chapter 3 — Bible Numerology and the Bible Code

1. A good technical treatment of legitimate biblical numerology can be found in Dr. William White's article in *Zondervan Pictorial Encyclopedia of the Bible,* Merrill C. Tenney, ed. (Grand Rapids: Zondervan, 1975), q.v. "Number," vol. 4., pp. 452-61.
2. Walter A. Elwell, *Evangelical Dictionary of Theology* (Grand Rapids: Baker, 1984).
3. *Zondervan Pictorial Encyclopedia of the Bible,* Merrill C. Tenney, ed. (Grand Rapids: Zondervan, 1975), vol. 4, p. 460.
4. John J. Davis, *Biblical Numerology* (Grand Rapids: Baker, 1995), chapters 3-4.
5. Ibid., pp. 110-11.
6. Ibid., pp. 127-28.
7. Ibid., pp. 129-30.
8. Ibid., pp. 112-13.
9. Robert Morey, *Bible Numerics: Fact or Fantasy?* (Newport, PA: Truth Seekers, 1997 ms. copy).
10. Davis, pp 137-44.
11. Ibid., p. 133.
12. Ibid., p. 134.
13. Ibid., p. 140.
14. Ibid., pp. 15, 146.
15. Ibid.
16. Morey, *Bible Numerics.*
17. Davis, pp. 148-49.
18. Ibid., p. 122.
19. Ibid., p. 155.
20. Ibid., p. 132.
21. "Today," transcript, May 29, 1997, p. 14.
22. Drosnin, p. 11.
23. Ibid., pp. 11-12.
24. *USA Today,* June 4, 1997, p. 8d.
25. Public statement by Harold Gans, June 3, 1997, Internet document.
26. Public statement by Doron Witztum, Internet document, June 4, 1997.
27. Public statement by Eliyahu Rips, June 4, 1997, Internet document.
28. *USA Today,* June 4, 1997, p. 8d.
29. *USA Today,* June 4, 1997.
30. Ibid.
31. Ronald S. Hendel, "The Secret Code Hoax," *Bible Review,* August 1997, p. 23.
32. Shlomo Sternberg, "Snake Oil for Sale," *Bible Review,* August 1994, p. 25; Wittes, "Cracking God's Code."

33. "Mathematician Critical of 'Bible Code' Bestseller," CNN Interactive World News story page, June 4, 1997, Internet document.

34. Public statement by Doron Witztum, Jerusalem, June 4, 1997, Internet document.

Chapter 4 — Hidden Codes: Only in the Bible?

1. Drosnin. p. 26.
2. Ibid., p. 29.
3. Ibid., p. 30.
4. Ibid., p. 192.
5. Ibid.
6. Ibid., p. 193.
7. Ibid.
8. Ibid., p. 32.
9. Peter Coy, "He Who Mines Data May Strike Fool's Gold," *Business Week*, June 16, 1997, p. 40, Internet document.
10. *Newsweek*, June 9, 1997, p. 66.
11. Sharon Begley, "Seek and Ye Shall Find," *Newsweek*, June 9, 1997, p. 66.
12. D. Trull, "Cracking the Bible Code," Internet document at *dtrull@periscope.com*, 1997.
13. *Newsweek*, June 9, 1997, p. 67.
14. Shlomo Sternberg, "Snake Oil for Sale," *Bible Review*, August 1997, p. 25.
15. Ibid.
16. *Newsweek*, June 9, 1997, p. 67.
17. Ibid.
18. Satinover, pp.195-96.
19. Ibid., p. 208.
20. Ibid., p. 209.
21. Ibid., pp. 209-10.
22. Ibid., p. 210.
23. Ibid., p. 216.
24. Ibid., p. 217.
25. Ibid., p. 9.
26. Ibid., p. 221.
27. Ibid., p. 207.
28. Ibid., p. 16.
29. See, for example, the relevant works of Richard Swineburne, especially his trilogy of Alvin Plantinga, and the text *Cosmos Bios Theos*, Henry Margenau, ed.
30. Ibid., pp. 14, 249, 251.
31. Ibid., p. 259.

Chapter 5 — Interpreting the Code: Some Key Dilemmas

1. Drosnin, p. 25.
2. Ibid.
3. Ibid., p. 45.
4. Ibid., p.102.
5. "The Oprah Winfrey Show," June 11, 1997, transcript p. 14, emphasis added.
6. Jeffrey B. Satinover, *Cracking the Bible Code* (New York: William Morrow & Co., 1997), p. 183.
7. Ibid., p. 238 (emphasis in original).
8. Ibid., p. 242 (emphasis added).
9. For example, Satinover, pp. 243-45.
10. Ibid., p. 244.
11. Drosnin, p. 91.
12. Ibid., p. 122.

13. Ibid.
14. Ibid., p. 122.
15. *USA Today,* June 4, 1997.
16. Davis, *Newsweek,* June 9, 1997, p. 143.
17. "Quabbalah," *The Encyclopedia of Religion,* (New York: Macmillan, 1987), vol. 12, p. 122.
18. Satinover, p. 89.
19. Ibid., p. 43.
20. Ibid., p. 44.
21. Ibid., p. 71.
22. Ibid.
23. Drosnin, p. 217.
24. Ibid., p. 105.
25. Ibid., p. 101.
26. Ibid.
27. Ibid.
28. Ibid., p. 95.
29. Ibid., p. 96.
30. Ibid., p. 17.
31. Shlomo Sternberg, "Snake Oil for Sale," *Bible Review,* August 1997, p. 25.
32. Drosnin, p.194.
33. Hendel, "The Secret Code Hoax," *Bible Review,* August 1997, p. 23.
34. "The Oprah Winfrey Show," June 11, 1997, p. 12, emphasis added.
35. "Hidden Codes in the Bible: Hoax or Prophecy?" Internet paper from OCRT Home Page, Christianity menu or "religious and ethical systems" menu.
36. Satinover, p. 143.
37. Ibid., p. 211.
38. Ibid., p. 212.
39. Ibid., p. 224.
40. Ibid., p. 321.
41. Ibid., p. 212.
42. Ibid., p. 45.
43. Ibid., p. 51.
44. Ibid., p. 214.
45. Sternberg, p. 25.
46. Hendel, "The Secret Code Hoax," p. 24.
47. Drosnin, pp. 218-19.

Chapter 6 — Problems Within the Bible Code

1. Drosnin, p. 46.
2. Ibid., p. 185.
3. Ibid., p. 19.
4. Ibid., p. 26.
5. Ibid., pp. 44-45, emphasis added.
6. Ibid., pp. 45-46.
7. Jeffrey B. Satinover, *Cracking the Bible Code* (New York: William Morrow & Co., 1997), pp. 45, 160, 259.
8. Ibid., p. 57.
9. Drosnin, p. 44.
10. Satinover, p. 17.
11. Ibid., p. 18.
12. Ibid., pp. 196-97.
13. R. Daniel Mechanic, in consultation with Doron Witztum and Harold Gans, "Jesus Codes: Uses and Abuses—A response to Yacov Rambsel and Grant Jeffrey," Internet document, no page numbers, second emphasis added. (*See* chapter 7, note 3.)

14. Drosnin, pp. 165-68, emphasis added.
15. Ibid., p. 142.
16. Drosnin, p. 170.
17. Ibid., p. 163.
18. Ibid., p. 173.
19. Ibid., p. 174.
20. Ibid.
21. Ibid.
22. Ibid.
23. Ibid., p. 182.
24. Ibid., p. 92.
25. Ibid., p. 96.
26. Ibid., p. 141.
27. Ibid., p. 164.
28. Ibid.
29. "Hidden Codes in the Bible: Hoax or Prophecy," Internet document.
30. "The Bible Code Cracked and Crumbling," *Bible Review*, August 1997, p. 22, cf. Rips. et al pp. 431, 435, where they claim "our definition of distance is not unique."
31. Drosnin, p. 96.
32. Wilner, Internet document.
33. Example cited from Sharon Begley, "Seek and Ye Shall Find" *Newsweek*, June 9, 1997, p. 67.
34. Transcript, June 11, 1997, p. 17.
35. Coy, p. 40.
36. *USA Today*, June 4, 1997, p. 8d.
37. Public statement, June 14, 1997, Internet document.
38. *USA Today*, June 4, 1997.
39. Dennis Eisenberg, "Bibliomancy," *Jerusalem Post*, August 1, 1997, p. 20 (emphasis added).
40. Begley, *Newsweek*, June 9, 1997, p. 67.
41. Satinover, p. 17.
42. Ibid., pp. 247, 324.
43. Ibid., p. 155.
44. Ibid., p. 292.
45. Ibid., p. 294.
46. Drosnin, p. 44.
47. Eisenberg, "Bibliomancy," p. 20, emphasis added.
48. Satinover, p. 250.
49. Ibid.

Chapter 7 — The Dangers of the Bible Code

1. Grant R. Jeffrey, *The Signature of God*, (Toronto, Canada: Frontier Publications, 1996) pp. 223, 225.
2. See note 3.
3. R. Daniel Mechanic, in consultation with Doron Witztum and Harold Gans, "Jesus Codes: Uses and Abuses—A Response to Yacov Rambsel and Grant Jeffery." This is a copy of an Internet article sent to Dr. Weldon without publication data or numbered pages. Here is their ELS data: The encoded word "Koresh" begins with the 34,103rd letter of Genesis located in chapter 24; the encoded word "Buddha" begins with the 53,479th letter of Genesis located in chapter 36; the encoded word "Shakran" begins with the 40,528th letter of Genesis located in chapter 29; the encoded word "Yeshua" begins with the 60,706th letter of Leviticus; the encoded word "Maysit" begins with the 24,350th letter of Exodus; the encoded word "Yeshua" begins with the 15,137th letter of Leviticus; the encoded word "Maysit" begins with the 5,859th letter of Leviticus; the encoded word "Mechashaif" begins with the 14,008th letter of Leviticus; "Yeshua" and "false prophet" are both encoded at the following skip distances in Genesis: 1,061; 4,379; 6,750; 9,381; 11,170; for example, begin-

ning with the 31,343rd letter of Genesis located in chapter 24 at a jump of plus 1,061 letters is the encoded word "Yeshua"; beginning with the 34,771st letter of Genesis located in
chapter 26 at a jump of -1,061 letters is the encoded word "false prophet." "Incredibly"
these two codes overlap; the encoded word "Mohammed" begins with the 5,892nd letter
letter of Genesis located in chapter 5; the encoded word "Krishna" begins with the 15,630th
letter of Deuteronomy; the encoded word "Buddha" begins with the 15,432nd letter of Genesis located in chapter 13; the encoded word "Koresh" begins with the 3,687th letter of Genesis located in chapter 27.

4. Robert Morey, Bible Numerics: Fact or Fantasy? (Newport, PA: Truth Seekers, 1997 ms.
copy).

5. Jeffrey B. Satinover, Cracking the Bible Code (New York: William Morrow & Co., 1997), p. 16.

6. Drosnin, The Bible Code (New York: Simon & Schuster, 1997), p. 116.

7. Ibid., pp. 63-64, 77.

8. Ibid., pp.61-65.

9. Ibid., p. 67.

10. Ibid., p. 68. Actually, Peres' statement was an indirect reference, not a "clear restatement."

11. Ibid., p. 81.

12. Ibid., p. 159.

13. Ibid., p. 161.

14. Ibid., p. 159.

15. "CBS This Morning," June 13, 1997, transcript p. 39.

16. Satinover, pp. 12, 131.

17. Ibid., p. 16.

18. See John Ankerberg and John Weldon, The Facts on UFOs and Other Supernatural Phenomena (Eugene, OR: Harvest House, 1995); cf. note 20.

19. Morris A. Goldstein, "Cabala," Collier's Encyclopedia (New York: Macmillan, 1992), vol. 5,
p. 85.

20. K.P. Bland, "Kabbalah," Keith Crim, gen. ed., Abingdon Dictionary of Living Religions,
(Nashville: Abingdon, 1987), p. 395.

21. Collier's Encyclopedia, 1992, vol. 5, p. 85. Others apply the term to "received or traditional
lore."

22. For examples, see John Ankerberg and John Weldon, The Coming Darkness (Eugene, OR:
Harvest House, 1993), appendix G. The entirety of this book documents the dangers of
occult involvement.

23. Satinover, pp. 74, 119.

24. Encyclopedia Judaica, "Kabbalah" (Jerusalem: Keten Publishing, 1972), vol. 10, p. 622.

25. Satinover, p. 393.

26. Ibid., p. 94.

27. Ibid.

28. Ibid., p. 259.

29. Ibid., p. 177.

30. Ibid., pp. 248-49.

31. Ibid., p. 100; see also pp. 94-97.

32. The Encyclopedia of Religion, Mircea Eliade, ed. (New York: Macmillan, 1987). The Cabala
therefore was considered the received or traditional lore, "Eliyyahu Ben Shelomah Zalman"
p. 99. Also, "Eliyahu became one of the major intellectual and spiritual figures in Judaism,
the preeminent representative of Rabbinism in the eighteenth century. At an early age, he
displayed a prodigious memory and a striking aptitude for analysis which he applied to all
branches of Jewish Law—the Torah, Mishreh, Talmud, Nidrash, Rabbinic Codes, and
Qabala. . . . the Gaon was a student of Jewish mysticism and he had an exceptionally vivid
visionary life. . . . His writings, including notes and jottings . . . were published by his dis-
ciples after his death. These include . . . glosses on the Zohar, Sefer Yetsirah, and other
Qabalistic classics" (vol. 12, pp. 98-100).

33. "The Mystic Life of the Gaon of Vilna" (Appendix F) in R.J. Zwi Werblowsky, *Joseph Karo: Lawyer and Mystic*, (Oxford: Oxford University Press, 1962), Scripta Judaica IV.

34. Drosnin, p. 19.

35. Satinover, p. 2.

36. Ibid., p. 173.

37. John Ankerberg and John Weldon, *Encyclopedia of New Age Beliefs*, chapter on divination.

38. *See* John Ankerberg and John Weldon, *Encyclopedia of New Age Beliefs* (Eugene, OR: Harvest House, 1996), pp. 34-39, 92-106, 110-12, 543-50, 598-99 for documentation.

39. Satinover, p. 252.

40. Ibid., pp. 252-53.

41. Ibid., pp. 67, 74-77, 83, 119, 247, 250, 274-75.

42. Ibid., p. 67.

43. Ibid., p. 67-76.

44. Ibid., p. 247.

45. *Business Week*, June 16, 1997, p. 40.

46. Ibid.

47. Drosnin, p. 44.

48. Ibid., p. 188, emphasis added.

49. "The Oprah Winfrey Show," June 11, 1997, transcript, p. 17.

50. Public statement by Doron Witztum, "Official Torah Codes," June 4, 1997.

51. Public statement by Harold Gans, "Official Torah Codes," June 3, 1997.

52. D. Trull, "Cracking the Bible Code."

53. Drosnin, pp. 158, 172-73.

54. "Mathematician Critical," CNN Interactive World News story page for June 4, 1997.

55. Satinover, p. 170.

56. Ibid., p. 173.

57. Ibid., p. 243-44.

58. Ibid., p. 243.

59. Ibid., p. 179.

60. John Ankerberg and John Weldon, *Encyclopedia of New Age Beliefs*, (Eugene, OR: Harvest House, 1996), pp. 124-25.

61. "The Oprah Winfrey Show," June 11, 1997, transcript, p. 15.

62. Ibid.

63. Drosnin, p. 103, emphasis added.

64. Ibid., p. 179.

65. Ibid.

66. Ibid., p. 103.

67. Ibid., p. 95.

68. Ibid., p. 97, emphasis added.

69. Ibid., pp. 97-98.

70. Clifford Wilson, *Close Encounters: A Better Explanation* (San Diego: Master Books, 1978); John Ankerberg and John Weldon, *The Facts on UFOs* (See chapter 7, note 20.)

71. Drosnin, pp. 94-98.

72. "NBC Today," May 29, 1997, transcript, p. 14.

Chapter 8 — Understanding the Kabbalah

1. *Encyclopedia Judaica*, "Kabbalah" (Jerusalem: Keten Publishing, 1972), vol. 10, p. 490.

2. "Mysticism, Jewish," *The Encyclopedia of Religion*, Mircea Eliade, gen. ed. (New York: Macmillan, 1987), vol. 12, p. 117.

3. *The Encyclopedia of Judaism*, Geoffrey Wigoder, gen. ed. (New York: Macmillan, 1989), p. 512.

4. *The Encyclopedia of Religion*, vol. 12, pp. 117-18.

5. Daniel Chanan Matt, *Zohar: The Book of Enlightenment* (New York, Paulist), 1983, p. 29.

6. Ibid.

7. *Encyclopedia Judaica,* vol. 10, p. 637.

8. *The Encyclopedia of Religion,* vol. 12, p.118.

9. Ibid.

10. *Encyclopedia Judaica,* vol. 10, p. 493.

11. Ibid., p. 632.

12. Ibid., p. 634.

13. Ibid., p. 633.

14. *See* John Ankerberg and John Weldon, *The Coming Darkness,* (Eugene, OR: Harvest House, 1993), chs. 2, 4 and appendices A-G.

15. Matt, p. 22.

16. Ibid.

17. Charles Poncé, *Kabbalah,* (Wheaton, IL: Theosophical Publishing House, 1978), pp. 94-95.

18. Ibid., pp. 95, 97.

19. *Encyclopedia Judaica,* vol. 10, p. 601.

20. Ibid.

21. Ibid., pp. 602-04.

22. Ibid., p. 605.

23. Poncé, p. 98.

24. *Encyclopedia Judaica,* vol. 10, p. 630.

25. *The Encyclopedia of Religion,* vol. 12, p. 121.

26. Poncé, pp. 98-99.

27. *The Encyclopedia of Judaism,* p. 512.

28. *Encyclopedia Judaica,* vol. 10, p. 624.

29. Ibid., pp. 620, 624.

30. Ibid., p. 622.

31. Ibid., p. 623.

32. Ibid.

33. *The Encyclopedia of Religion,* vol. 12, p. 122.

34. *Encyclopedia Judaica,* vol. 10, p. 623.

35. Jeffrey B. Satinover, *Cracking the Bible Code,* (William Morrow & Co., 1997), p. 353.

36. *See* John Ankerberg and John Weldon, *Darwin's Leap of Faith* (Eugene, OR: Harvest House, 1998).

37. Matt, p. 31.

38. Ibid.

39. Ibid., p. 23.

40. *Encyclopedia Judaica,* vol. 10, p. 494.

41. Matt, pp. 23-24.

42. Ibid., p. 30.

43. *The Encyclopedia of Religion,* vol. 12, pp. 123-44.

44. *Encyclopedia Judaica,* vol. 10, pp. 638-42.

Chapter 9 — The Clear Message of the Bible

1. Michael Shermer, "O Ye of Little Faith; *Cracking the Bible Code,* and Other 'Proofs' of God," *Skeptic,* vol. 5, no. 2, 1997, p. 55.

2. Citations were taken from John Ankerberg and John Weldon, *Ready with an Answer,* (Eugene, OR: Harvest House, 1997, pp. 292-93). We recommend this book for those interested in some of the reasons undergirding the Christian acceptance of the Bible as the Word of God from the perspective of biblical, archaeological, textual, historical, and scientific data.

3. For more on this, see *Knowing the Truth About Salvation* by John Ankerberg and John Weldon (Eugene, OR: Harvest House, 1996).